Economics in Crisis

Outline of an alternative

Other fine books from the same publisher:

The Traitor and The Jew, by Esther Delisle
Zen & the Art of Post-Modern Canada, by Stephen Schecter
The Last Cod Fish, by Pol Chantraine
Seven Fateful Challenges for Canada, by Deborah Coyne
*A Canadian Myth: Quebec, between Canada and the
Illusion of Utopia,* by William Johnson
Devil's Advocate, by Patrice Dutil
Dead-End Democracy? by Yves Leclerc
Voltaire's Man in America, by Jean-Paul de Lagrave
Judaism: From the Religious to the Secular, by A.J. Arnold

Canadian Cataloguing in Publication Data

Rochon, Louis-Philippe
  Economics in crisis : outline of an alternative
  Includes bibliographical references

  ISBN 2-895854-16-4

  1. Keynesian economics   2. Economic Policy   3. Tax and expenditure limitations.   4. Unemployment.   5. Inflation (Finance).   I. Title

HB98.7.R62 1994   330.15'6   C94-941251-1

This is the 5th book to appear in the Food for Thought series

If you would like to receive our current catalogue and announcements
of new titles, please send your name and address to:
ROBERT DAVIES PUBLISHING,
P.O. Box 702, Outremont, Quebec, Canada H2V 4N6

DISCARD
Economics
in Crisis

Outline of an Alternative

by Louis-Philippe Rochon

ROBERT DAVIES PUBLISHING
MONTREAL/TORONTO

This book may be ordered in Canada from
General Distribution Services,
☎ 1-800-387-0141 / 1-800-387-0172 FAX 1-416-445-5967.
In the U.S.A., toll-free 1-800-805-1083.
Or from the publisher, (514)481-2440, FAX (514)481-9973.

The publisher takes this opportunity to thank the
Canada Council and the Ministère de la Culture du Québec
for their continuing support.

Cover illustration: interpretation of a detail of
Diablito No. 3 (1962)
by René Portocarrero

"**There has been a fundamental misunderstanding**
of how . . . the economy in which we live
actually works."

John Maynard Keynes

CONTENTS

PREFACE

Economic news receives wide coverage, and, especially when the economy performs poorly, economic issues generate widespread political debate. Yet, the way we look at the economy—the state of economics—is seldom the issue it should be.

Despite differences among economists, the link between economic thought and the way economic problems are approached is neglected. Partly, this is because the language and techniques of the economics profession provide a formidable barrier to outsiders who want to know what is really going on. Often, debate among economists is thought to be best left to people far away in the "ivory tower," because it has little relevance to the real world.

In this book, Louis-Philippe Rochon renders two important services. First, he shows that the terms of the debate among economists can be understood by those outside the profession. Second, he demonstrates the important links between economic thought and economic policy.

Changing the way people think about the economy is no easy task, but new thinking is probably necessary if economic questions are to be addressed more successfully. Historically, changing circumstances *have* produced new thinking, which should be cause for some optimism, but rearguard action by protectors of the prevailing orthodoxy has often been effective in controlling its effects. Such was the case, for instance, for the thought of John Maynard Keynes, an important presence in *Economics in Crisis.*

As Rochon shows, the Keynesian revolution never succeeded in the sense of overthrowing the dominant tradition. Instead, we got the neo-classical "synthesis," which absorbed Keynes's thought as a "special case." While Keynes himself viewed the self-regulating market economy as prone to stagnation and high levels of unemployment, his successors continued to work with flexible-price models that assumed away the problems he had identified with the investment mechanism, the role of government, the non-neutrality of money, and the creation of employment. Mainstream views about issues discussed by Rochon, such as debt, inflation, and unemployment, give quite different answers than do the approach of the "bastard Keynesians."

In this work, the economic analysis offered by the neo-classical school is examined and found wanting. In its place, Rochon offers the views of the post-Keynesians. In his hands, the new approach gives some surprising and encouraging conclusions. Government debt may best be understood as the necessary counterpart to a society wishing to invest in education, health, and social services, not a burden on future generations. Inflation may be the result of the struggle among different groups for a large share of income, not the consequences of over-spending by government. Unemployment can be thought of as a social issue that can be eliminated through government policies.

The courage to think differently from the currently influential and powerful is something to be admired, particularly when it is done well. Indeed, it may be the "scarce good" so helpful to standard economic analysis of supply and demand. In his work, Rochon has drawn on some of the most interesting work in contemporary economics, much of it being done by Canadians. I would like to see a copy of this book in the hands of all those who embark on a university course in the social sciences. After all, as the saying goes, to be forewarned is to be forearmed.

Duncan Cameron

Duncan Cameron teaches political economy at the University of Ottawa. He is editor of the Canadian Forum *and president of the Canadian Centre for Policy Alternatives.*

INTRODUCTION

Economics is in a complete shambles, with the collapse of economic theory and policy that followed the disastrous experience of the 1980s. The mainstream theories can no longer justify the policies that dominated the last decade. Although there appears to be less consensus today on the economic policies adopted since the early 1980s, they nonetheless remain the established orthodoxy.[1] Following the failure of traditional Keynesian policies to explain the dismal performance of the economy in the early 1970s, a theoretical void paved the way for the resurgence of an even stronger version of the pre-Keynesian ideology of free-market enterprise and self-regulating markets.

Milton Friedman, who won the 1976 Nobel Prize for his contribution to economic theory, influenced politicians and economists around the world in the 1970s with his vision of how to combat inflation and unemployment. His proposed policies were heralded as a panacea for economic woes, and the era of neoconservatism was born. Because of the relative simplicity of his monetary policy, central banks were quickly seduced by Friedman's tenets, and his academic reputation and accomplishments convinced governments the world over to cut back on their activist fiscal policies. This enthusiasm was not universal, however; Friedman has been called the "Lysenko of economics."[2]

The Friedman-influenced 1980s were a failure on all counts. Far from improving, the economic climate actually worsened. Friedman's policies proved to be destructive, and many economists are now taking great pains to distance themselves from them. Nonetheless, his thought remains the inevitable orthodoxy.

In terms of economic policy, the last fifteen years have proved to be among the worst in Canada's history: Canadians have lived through two major recessions, unemployment has risen considerably and remains at unacceptably high levels, incomes have polarized, and productivity and living standards have declined. The combination of policies of economic austerity, privatization, and free trade have had a detrimental effect not only on the economy as a whole but on our individual lives as well. Clearly, there is a crisis.

The problem with present-day economics is that there is little consensus on the causes of economic cycles, the severity of the problems at hand, and the solutions that should be pursued. Economic theory is divided along certain ideological and methodological lines, and each camp has its own set of ideas, ideals, and philosophy. This "baggage" influences not only how economists see the world, but how they would like it to operate. To believe that economics is objective is at best naïve, since it allows ideology to pass for science. In fact, "No social science or particular branch of social research can ever be 'neutral' or simply 'factual,' indeed not 'objective' in the traditional meaning of the terms. Research is always and by logical necessity based on moral or political valuations, and the researcher should be obliged to account for them explicitly."[3]

Policy makers are also influenced by ideology, either directly or through their advisers. Government economic policies—or the lack thereof—are a measure of faith in a particular vision of the world. In the last fifteen years or so, there has been a trend throughout the world to espouse free enterprise and market-oriented economic policies, reflecting a faith in the supreme functioning of markets and their ability to solve our economic woes. Neoconservatism, as this new orthodoxy is called, is based on a set of economic axioms, principles, postulates, theories, and philosophies called neoclassical. In a sense, therefore, "There appears to be an economic crisis in the real world which is not unrelated to the crisis in economic theory. For this economic crisis . . . is being precipitated by policy advice derived from irrelevant schools of neoclassical economic thought."[4] During the economic crisis of the 1930s, politicians were talking about fiscal prudence, balanced budgets, credit controls, and wage roll-backs. These policies were unable to solve—and, indeed, unnecessarily prolonged—the problems of the depression, and so it is not surprising that they cannot deal with today's more complex world. As long as policy makers rely on neoclassical philosophy, there is little doubt that the economy will continue to sputter.

Economic theory is vital to policy makers. It shapes their choice of problems to address (for instance, inflation rather than unemployment) and their use of tools to resolve these problems (for instance, high interest rates rather than fiscal policies). These decisions are, in turn, based partly on economics and partly on self-interest. Policies affect people and groups directly and differently; income distribution must therefore be a central component of economic theory.

It is a contemporary fact that those who have more power are able to influence governments to adopt policies that benefit them. For instance, the high-interest-rate policy of the Friedman years has benefited the rentiers, while harming entrepreneurs and workers, and the neoconservative austerity policies implemented in the 1980s continue to dominate, to the detriment of certain parts of society, because "the goal of restrictive monetary and fiscal policy as anti-inflation devices is to weaken the various domestic and foreign groups . . . by creating business losses and unemployment [so] that they will not have the strength to continue the struggle. Unfortunately, those that are most likely to be weakened are those with the least power to begin with."[5] Or, put another way, "Left to themselves, economic forces do not work out for the best except perhaps for the powerful."[6]

To be viable, an economy must be able to meet the basic needs of its citizens and replace the capital stock used during the process of production. Any surplus wealth is divided up between various classes or groups, and this distribution is determined by the power relationship between workers, capital owners, and rentiers. Those who can influence policies will be in a position to extract a larger share of the surplus wealth.

Although economic theory contains many schools of thought, this book will be concentrating essentially on only two (the most important ones): neoclassical and post-Keynesian (based on the writings of British economist John Maynard Keynes and of those he influenced). It should be mentioned from the start that neoclassical theory has been the dominant school of thought since its inception, in the nineteenth century, although post-Keynesian influence is growing, especially in the face of the current crisis. Differences between these two schools of thought are not limited to the fact that they provide different answers to the same old questions. In fact, post-Keynesian and other heterodox theories seek to ask different questions altogether: "The differences between post-Keynesian and neoclassical economics are not so much the difference in their subject matter as they are differences in their treatment of economic life."[7]

The economic policies promulgated by each school are constrained by their respective methodologies. The economist's perception of the "merits of a particular research . . . is to some extent the result of her inborn predispositions and economic environment. More specifically, the economist's 'world view' reflects her personal stock of knowledge resultant from past choices of reading from the available literature."[8] As well, economists' view of the world and their philosophical and ideological penchants cannot be separated, as each feeds the other, and the confidence that they have in their policy recommendations is primarily ideological. "There is no such thing as a 'purely economic' problem that can be settled by purely economic logic; political interests and political prejudice are involved in every discussion of actual questions."[9] In other words, every "comprehensive 'theory' of an economic state of society consists of two complementary but essentially distinct elements. There is, first, the theorist's view about the basic features of that state of society, about what is and what is not important in order to understand its life at a given time. Let us call this his vision. And there is, second, the theorist's technique, an apparatus by which he conceptualizes his vision and which turns the latter into concrete propositions on 'theories.'"[10] Thus, facts can be observed and interpreted and hypotheses tested in different ways. For instance, while unemployment is currently very high, neoclassical economists observe that it is near its "natural" level and feel that there is no urgent need to address the problem; therefore, they would recommend that issues such as inflation be attacked instead.

Economists' vision of the world influences not only how they see and address particular problems, but also the questions they seek to answer. They thus become "propagandists of values."[11] In other words, facts do not "organize themselves into concepts and theories just by being looked at. . . . Questions must be asked before answers can be given. The questions are an expression of our interest in the world"[12]—and of the degree of our objectivity. This explains why neoclassical economists are not interested in persistent unemployment, class struggles, and income distribution, and why their theories contain few—or no—inferences to these questions.

Since the current economic crisis is related to the dominance of neoconservative policies based on neoclassical theory, the obvious solution is to reject them, and to replace them with another set of principles and ideals. The aim of this book is to provide a credible alternative to the dominant paradigm in economic theory. I do not claim to provide detailed solutions to all of our problems; that is the stuff of more profound research and much thicker books. There is, however, a need to inform Canadians of the existence of other theories and to try to convince them that post-Keynesian economic theory forms "an integral whole, thereby demonstrating that it is just as comprehensive and coherent"[13] as neoclassical theory. Having been told that there is no alternative to government fiscal restraint, Canadians have accepted the idea that deficits are a sign of our failure as a society, and that there is no longer a legitimate role for governments to play in economic growth and job creation. We are constantly told that governments should not interfere by creating employment; this should be left to the private sector and to market forces, which are best served when they are freed from the shackles of government regulation. The last fifteen years, however, do not seem to confirm the credibility of this philosophy. In fact, if left to themselves, markets will never lead—even in the best of times—to full employment. This is the reality of modern capitalism, and it is why activist fiscal policies should be pursued.

This book deals with economic myths. Although it focuses on three major ones—debt, inflation, and unemployment—it also touches on others, including interest rates, prices, and wages. First, however, two chapters trace the main ideas of John Maynard Keynes and of neoclassical theory. I felt that this was necessary because Keynes himself is at the centre of the greatest myth of all. Many economists and politicians blame him and the policies that were inspired by his writings for the current economic fiasco and claim that the extravagant policies adopted after the Second World War are responsible for today's high deficits and debt. As well, these two introductory chapters shed light on the unsound hypotheses upon which neoclassical theory is based.

The overall objective of this book is not to plead a cause or an ideology; nor is it to attack or denigrate. Rather, it is to clarify the complex and evolving realities of the capitalist system that shapes our lives, and to elucidate the policy implications they hold. I do not wish to condemn capitalism for what it has done, but for what it has failed to do. The task of convincing Canadians of the validity of an alternative economic approach is a difficult one. Those of us who espouse this alternative are painted as radicals or, even worse, as enemies of Canada. Yet the effort must be undertaken, for we are seriously discussing the future of our country. While this book is primarily addressed to non-academic Canadians, I hope that it will also be read by students and by fellow economists, who seldom have the courage to peek beyond their textbooks.

INTRODUCTION

This book is the result of my own "long struggle," in Keynes's words, to understand why orthodox economic theory has not been able to solve the problems of society. The process has sometimes been long and laborious, but it has also been rewarding and challenging. As an undergraduate student, I remember learning all the graphs, curves, formulas, and theories that, we were told, governed markets and individual behaviour. I remember thinking that this was absurd, life could not possibly be this meticulous, but I did not possess the necessary tools to criticize what Flaubert called *"les idées reçues."* It was only during my third year at university that I finally started to piece together the various elements of my criticism. I realized that the answers had been there all along, but that the professors chose to ignore them by teaching theories exclusively from the school of neoclassical economic thought. From then on, I began to explore the alternatives.

During my academic adventure, I have acquired many intellectual debts. In particular, I would like to thank Professor Marc Lavoie, of the University of Ottawa, for having started me on my current journey. Without his "Introduction to Post-Keynesian Theory," I surely would have become a slave to orthodoxy. His eye-opening analysis and clarity of thought have stayed with me, and his influence is evident throughout this book. My thesis supervisor at McGill University, the late and much-missed Professor Athanasios Asimakopulos, inspired me to look beyond appearances, and his reading of Keynes greatly influenced mine. I would also like to thank Mario Seccareccia, of the University of Ottawa, and Robin Rowley, of McGill University, whose friendship I greatly value; their repeated advice was always considered and often followed. As well, my two years of lecturing at the University of Ottawa have allowed me to benefit from casual conversation and heated debates with a number of my colleagues. Finally, I would like to thank those who read earlier drafts of my book and offered their comments and suggestions. Of course, they are not responsible for any mistakes or misinterpretations that may appear herein.

Just as crucial has been my ongoing association with the magazine *Cité libre* as a member of the editorial board, which has allowed me to think out loud about some of the important links between disparate elements. My regular articles, which have sparked debates with readers and discussions with members of the editorial board in that cozy living room on Parc Lafontaine Street in Montreal, have enabled me to fine-tune my thoughts. I would like to thank in particular Anne-Marie Bourdouxhe, the editor-in-chief, for publishing my articles despite their sometimes obscure nature.

Finally, I am especially grateful to Tyrone Newhook, an aspiring journalist, for his editing and critical advice. As he frequently reminded me, academics do not know how to write, and he is probably correct. A final thanks to my publisher and close friend, Robert Davies, for accepting the manuscript.

Notes

1. The words "orthodox," "mainstream," and "neoclassical" will be used interchangeably throughout.
2. See Lavoie and Seccareccia, *Milton Friedman*. Trofim Denisovich Lysenko (1898–1976) was a Russian biologist and agronomist who was president of the Lenin All-Union Academy of Agricultural Sciences and the scientific and administrative leader of Soviet agriculture. Lysenko later became the leader of the Soviet School of Genetics, which opposed the theories of heredity and supported the doctrine that characteristics acquired through environmental influences are inherited. Based on his theoretical beliefs, he was convinced that corn could be grown in Siberia.
3. Myrdal, *Objectivity in Social Research*, p. 74.
4. Davidson, "Post Keynesian Economics," p. 151.
5. Ibid., p. 163.
6. Galbraith, *Economics and the Public Purpose*, p. xii.
7. Shapiro, "The Revolutionary Character," p. 552.
8. Dow and Earl, "Methodology and Orthodox," p. 145.
9. J. Robinson, "What are the Questions?," p. 1318.
10. Schumpeter, *Ten Great Economists*, p. 268.
11. Bonin, "L'analyse économique," p. 12.
12. Myrdal, *Political Element,* p. vii.

13. Eichner, *Toward a New Economics*, p. 3.

Economics in crisis

C H A P T E R   O N E

JOHN MAYNARD KEYNES

John Maynard Keynes (1883–1946), considered the father of modern macro-economics, left a significant intellectual legacy, covering not only economics and political economy, but calculus, probability, philosophy, and psychology. After starting a career as a public servant, he returned to Cambridge University in 1908, where he had done his undergraduate work, at the request of his former professor and mentor, Alfred Marshall, to be a lecturer in economics. Three years later, at the age of twenty-eight, he became the editor of *The Economic Journal*, a very influential and prominent position. Despite his success as an economist, however, Keynes was not content with the tranquil life of academe and rapidly became involved in political life in England.[1] He became a renowned financial investor and was an advisor to the British government during the First World War, an influential figure at important international gatherings, and one of the architects of the Bretton Woods system, which in 1944 set up the International Monetary Fund and the World Bank.

Keynes's vast and varied interests gave him a first-hand look how the real world operated. Intrigued by what he saw, he set out to devise a theory that would better reflect the workings of a modern capitalist economy, in which money and uncertainty played a prominent and central role. His best-known book is *The General Theory of Employment, Interest and Money*,[2] published in 1936, which was primarily a study of the causes of unemployment. A work of tremendous importance, it was meant as a direct attack on the dominant orthodox school of thought. Keynes's approach was radically different from that of his colleagues, and so was his vision of the world.

In the opening paragraph of the *General Theory*, Keynes explained the use of the word "general" in its title. According to him, neoclassical theory and the world in which it supposedly existed comprised only one particular case, while his own vision of the world, in which unemployment is a permanent feature, was the more general case: "The object of such a title is to contrast the character of my arguments and conclusions with those of the [neo]*classical* theory of the subject. . . . Moreover, the characteristics of the special case assumed by the classical theory happen not to be those of the economic society in which we live."[3]

The *General Theory* was a response to the poor performance of the British economy. Keynes started working on the book in 1932, when England was ten years into a severe recession. The accompanying prolonged period of massive unemployment was somewhat of a puzzle, since the dominant theories of the day posited that unemployment could only be temporary; provided that everyone was motivated by self-interest and that all individuals and firms were acting rationally, the economy would, on its own, guarantee full employment and stable prices. Obviously, the "facts of experience," as Keynes put it, did not give credence to this view. It was to oppose this "invisible hand"[4] that Keynes wrote the *General Theory*. He never hid his disenchantment with Smithian *laissez-faire* philosophy:

> Let us be clear from the ground the metaphysical or general principles upon which, from time to time, *laissez-faire* has been founded. It is *not* true that individuals possess a prescriptive "natural liberty" in their economic activities. There is *no* "compact" conferring perpetual rights on those who Have or on those who Acquire. The world is *not* governed from above so that private and social interest always coincide. It is *not* managed here below that in practice they coincide. It is *not* a correct deduction from the principles of economics that enlightened self-interest generally *is* enlightened; more often individuals acting separately to promote their own needs are too ignorant or too weak to attain even these. Experience does *not*

show that individuals when they make up a social unit, are always less clear-sighted than when they act separately.[5]

The consequences of the *laissez-faire* philosophy were not to be underestimated; according to Keynes, it was a dangerous enterprise in capitalist and democratic societies. As he noted in chapter one of the *General Theory*, the teaching of neoclassical theory is "misleading and disastrous if we attempt to apply it to the facts of experience."[6]

Keynes's goal with the *General Theory* was to change the way economists and policy makers perceived the actual world, based on his experience in public life, which gave him a clear understanding of the workings of a capitalist economy of production. His attack was aimed at the economists and policy makers of his day who clung to the assumptions of neoclassical theory, which, he felt, did not take into consideration crucial elements of reality.

In a letter to George Bernard Shaw, dated 1 January 1935, Keynes did not conceal his enthusiasm for what he believed was to be a true revolution. In contrasting his own work with Karl Marx's "unsuitable" *Das Kapital*, he wrote, "To understand my new state of mind, however, you have to know that I believe myself to be writing a book on economic theory which will largely revolutionize not I suppose at once but in the course of the next ten years the way the world thinks about economic problems. I can't expect you or anyone else to believe this at the present stage, but for myself I don't merely hope what I say. In my own mind, I am quite sure."[7]

In the *General Theory*, Keynes emphasized that his "controversial passages are aimed at providing some material for an answer . . . [to the] lack of clearness and generality [of neoclassical theory]."[8] Despite his best intentions, though, the *General Theory* remains a difficult book to read, partly because of the complex nature of his ideas and concepts, and partly because he failed to "work everything out in a consistent manner."[9] Certain ideas expressed in it are inconsistent with his own treatment of them elsewhere in his body of work—and even in previous drafts of the

General Theory itself. He more or less conceded his lack of clarity when he stated that economists often write in a "quasi-formal style; and there can be no doubt, in spite of the disadvantages, that this is our best available means of conveying our thoughts to one another. But when an economist writes in a quasi-formal style, he is composing neither a document verbally complete and exact so as to be capable of a strict legal interpretation, nor a logically complete proof. Whilst it is his duty to make his premises and his use of terms as clear as he can, he never states all his premises and his definitions perfectly clear-cut."[10]

Another problem may be that for years Keynes believed in neoclassical theory, the very theory he set out to discredit in the *General Theory*. As he points out in the preface, "I myself held with conviction for many years the theories which I now attack, and I am not, I think ignorant of their strong points."[11] A few pages later, he candidly admits that the "composition of this book has been for the author a long struggle to escape . . . from the habitual modes of thought and expression. . . . The difficulty lies, not in the new ideas but in escaping from the old ones, which ramify, for those brought up as most of us have been, into every corner of our minds."[12] Unfortunately, at the time he wrote the *General Theory*, Keynes was not as completely free from his attachment to *laissez-faire* as he thought. After it was completed, he was unhappy with some sections and felt that "doubtless some details are obscure, incomplete, or wrong."[13] This ambivalence has made the book difficult to read and to interpret and has led many economists to try to understand what "Keynes really meant."

To comprehend the theoretical significance of the *General Theory*, it must therefore not be read in isolation, since it is only part of a larger, more "general" theory. By concentrating exclusively on this work, economists may be misled into drawing conclusions that, without the greater context of Keynes's entire theory, may actually contradict his policy prescriptions. Unfortunately, most economists have ignored his other writings. The consequence, as we will see, has been the adoption of "Keynesian" policies that find little theoretical support in Keynes's writings.

From a historical perspective, Keynes will certainly be regarded as the most influential economist of the twentieth century. His *General Theory* ranks among the most important works to be published on economics, on a par with Adam Smith's *Wealth of Nations*, David Ricardo's *Principles*, and Karl Marx's *Das Kapital*. Unlike these other works, the *General Theory* continues to generate heated and controversial debate within academic and political circles; even his ideological adversaries have recognized the profound influence Keynes has had on economic thought and policy.

One of Keynes's main criticisms was that market economies do not tend naturally toward full employment. This has been recognized all over the world—for instance, in the American Employment Act of 1946, in the new French Constitution of 1946, in Article 55 of the Charter of the United Nations, and in Article 104 of the Rome Treaty. "None of this would have occurred without the appearance of Keynes's *General Theory*—since maintaining full employment would not have occurred to economists or politicians as a feasible policy objective"[14] in a world in which markets were thought to guarantee full employment naturally.

Research on "what Keynes really meant" was for a long time limited to economists and academics who knew him well—the "fundamentalist Keynesians." Economists' interest in Keynes was stimulated by the publication in 1973 of *The Collected Writings of John Maynard Keynes*, a thirty-volume set of his articles, philosophy, and correspondence.[15] Currently, economists studying Keynes are called post-Keynesians. Their research is not limited to Keynes, although they are still greatly influenced by his writings; their objective is to develop a coherent, credible alternative to the current orthodox ideas, while always remembering that realism defines the foundations for theorizing.

Keynes's Main Contributions to Economic Theory

Uncertainty and Expectations

The concept of uncertainty predates Keynes. In 1921, an entire book was dedicated to it. In *Risk, Uncertainty and Profit,* Frank Knight claims that if "we are to understand the workings of the economic system we must examine the meaning and significance of uncertainty. . . . [We cannot] infer the future from the present with any high degree of dependability, nor yet do we accurately know the consequences of our own actions."[16]

Uncertainty is the most important element in Keynes's economic theory; it permeates his writings. He sought to explain the workings of a contemporary market economy subject to fluctuations in investment, and to understand the reasons for economic downturns and booms by investigating what causes investment to be so volatile. According to Keynes, the answer lies with the existence of uncertainty, which can influence not only the growth rate of the economy but its direction as well. In a capitalist system, uncertainty instils dynamic forces that make the system unstable. Because of uncertainty and external shocks, Keynes did not see capitalist economies as "self-adjusting" systems gravitating toward a "natural" growth path, or toward any long-term level of employment or production.

What is uncertainty? This question has led to much debate in economics. For Keynes, uncertainty deals with the future, which, by definition, is unknown. Economic agents have no guarantee that realized results will be the ones anticipated, or that events will actually occur. For instance, a firm has no certain way of knowing whether its investment will be profitable; similarly, workers cannot be certain that they will be employed even a few months hence. True uncertainty can influence motives and decisions in unforeseen ways; it is thus crucial to include it in economic theory.[17]

Keynes was clear on this point:

The outstanding fact is the extreme precariousness of the basis of knowledge on which our estimates of prospective yields have to be made. Our knowledge of the factors which will govern the yield on investment some years hence is usually very slight and often negligible. If we speak frankly, we have to admit that our basis of knowledge for estimating the yields ten years hence . . . amounts to little and sometimes nothing. . . . In fact, those who seriously attempt to make any such estimates are often so much in the minority that their behaviour does not govern the market.[18]

In a 1937 article in the *Quarterly Journal of Economics,* one year after publication of the *General Theory,* Keynes answered his critics by emphasizing once more the importance of uncertainty. He explained, "[I do] not mean merely to distinguish what is known for certain from what is only probable. The game of roulette is not subject, in this sense, to uncertainty. . . . The sense in which I am using the term is that . . . there is no scientific basis on which to form any calculable probability whatever." And he added, for emphasis, "We simply do not know."[19] Since, many economists have recognized the importance of uncertainty in economic theory. Even one very neoclassical economist called it "an innovation of sublime importance."[20]

The inclusion of uncertainty in economic theory is therefore important if we are to understand the problems of the real world. In the absence of knowledge of the future, economic agents—firms and households—act, react, and approach problems and situations differently, and they must rely on forecasts that may or may not be accurate. They base their behaviour on expectations of the future, near and far, and it is these expectations that drive the economy. Furthermore, it cannot be assumed all agents are identical and possess the same information. Since each firm and household has a different agenda, it is logical to assume that they will have different expectations of and reactions to identical situations. They can thus be said to make decisions based on the confidence they have in their own expectations—that is, their "subjective feeling of confidence."

Economic agents are social and historical entities, not atomistic ones. They exist in a society that conditions their behaviour and influences their decisions. Institutions and groups such as labour unions, educational and professional associations, capitalists, and rentiers play a vital part, influencing not only the decisions of their own members, but those of members of other groups as well.

Without perfect knowledge of the future, decisions by economic agents often rely on a variety of rules of thumb. This does not imply that they are irrational; quite the contrary. Given the existing level of information and the state of expectations, economic agents act according to the knowledge they possess. Their behaviour will be dictated not by cool, mathematical rationality, but by what I call historical rationality: what they know of the past and what they expect of the future. These rules of thumb become "modes of behavior that the firm (or individual) develops as guides for making decisions in a complex environment with uncertainty and incomplete information."[21]

Rules of thumb can take various forms. Three possibilities were suggested by Keynes:[22] economic agents can take the past as a guide to the future, hoping that repeated events will lead to repeated outcomes; they can assume that their expectations of the future are correct; or they can follow the opinions and decisions of the majority. It is the third rule of thumb that is perhaps the most often observed. By following actions of others, it implies, there is less of a chance of being wrong and the possibility of failure is minimized. For instance, if a firm is uncertain about the health of the economy in the future—that is, about the strength of effective demand—and does not know whether it should wait before going ahead with planned investment, it will look around to see what other firms are doing. This behaviour is actually quite rational, given the presence of uncertainty.

The importance of conventions and norms is therefore paramount when dealing with uncertainty, as individuals develop a sense of security when they follow beaten paths. Self-interest-maximizing behaviour is replaced by "satisficing" behaviour: individuals are willing to forgo certain situations in which uncertainty is high, despite greater potential profits, in favour of those that have already proven successful. The conclusion that can be drawn from this is dramatic: "When proceeding to analyze the overall economy, we can dispense with going into the intricate details of individual behaviour and content ourselves with the study of the interaction between the various groups and classes of society based on the received conventions."[23]

While there are other behavioural patterns,[24] the bottom line is that, when faced with uncertainty, the behaviour of economic agents is anything but predictable and mathematical. Despite the obvious presence of uncertainty, conventional neoclassical theorists refuse to incorporate this real-world element into their analysis. It is for this reason that Keynes referred to neoclassical theory as a "pretty, polite technique."[25]

The "Short Period" and Historical Time

Like uncertainty, the concept of time is very much neglected in economic theory, and especially in neoclassical models. However, until we deal explicitly with the concept of time, we "cannot analyze the concept of changes in the economic system."[26]

Neoclassical theory is rooted in an analysis of changes in economic variables in the "long run," in which time is nonexistent and variables are essentially not allowed to vary. This approach relies on a set of hypotheses that asks economists to have faith in a specific vision of the world. Keynes rejected this long-run approach, since he saw uncertainty as preventing the economy from moving toward any specific position at any point in time; rather, at best, it is moving from one unstable period to another without any specific resting place in mind. This may sound unscientific, and to some degree it is, but the existence of uncertainty makes the idea of a "natural" trajectory very unlikely. For this reason, Keynes rarely looked beyond the short term; when he did, it was not part of his formal analysis. The *General Theory* follows this prescription by studying the causes of unemployment over periods of actual time ranging from a few months to a year.

Keynes's "short period" is not self-contained, but is part of a temporal sequence. As the economy moves through time, economic agents do not have the luxury of starting over again when the desired results are not realized; they are stuck with what exists in the present. Scenarios always unfold along uncertain paths; since the development of the economy is path dependent, decisions to invest and consume have repercussions that drive the economy in unknown directions. A firm may invest today, but if consumers do not buy its product, the hoped-for results will not materialize. Therefore, entrepreneurs must constantly revise their strategies in the light of changing and unexpected circumstances. In other words, decisions "taken in the light of expectations or conventions in today's short-period situation are continually bringing into being a new short-period situation which is no nearer to equilibrium than yesterday's."[27] In this sense, the economy can be said to be moving in all directions at once, following a "kaleidoscopic" path;[28] in other words, "human societies are subject to continuous evolution the precise direction of which can never be predicted."[29] Thus, to develop a realistic analysis, it is necessary to get rid of the concept of long-run equilibrium and substitute historical time, in which the ever-moving present separates an irrevocable past from an uncertain future. This implies that decisions made today are influenced by both the past and the future, and that there is a historical component to any decision to consume or invest. Economic analysis must therefore consider the historical process through which the economy travels, constantly interacting with what Keynes called a "political, social, and natural environment." Keynes saw neoclassical theory as ignoring this "awkward fact."

Equilibrium
Equilibrium is another concept that has not been well understood by economists. In general, they have traditionally thought it to be

a position in which, given an initial set of conditions, the market price and quantity produced of a commodity tend not to change. In such a situation, consumers and producers have no tendency to change their respective demand and supply. Neoclassical economists add a more restrictive clause to this concept, which states that at the chosen market price, markets will "clear," meaning that quantity demanded will be exactly equal to quantity supplied. This approach is applied to all markets, including the labour market, which explains why neoclassical theorists do not believe that unemployment can exist. This concept of equilibrium is associated with the long run.

The notion of an uncertain future combined with Keynes's short-period analysis makes it obvious that the notion of an economy in long-run equilibrium is untenable in a world in which everything is moving at once. Equilibrium implies rest, and it can only exist in tranquil situations, which is contrary to Keynes's view of capitalism. In other words, "Uncertain expectations is wholly incompatible and in conflict with the notion of equilibrium."[30]

The challenge that Keynes posed to orthodox theory was this notion of equilibrium. For him, equilibrium was a completely different notion: a position of choice. Given the values of the parameters or the general conditions of the economy, firms would hire just enough labour to produce the output demanded at that point in time. In this sense, Keynes's view of the economy is closer to that of classical economists such as Ricardo and Marx: firms have simply "chosen" a certain level of output, and hence of employment; thus, according to Keynes, unemployment was also a position of equilibrium. Today, this notion is largely misunderstood by economists.

For Keynes, the economy could never be seen as moving toward a position of long-run equilibrium: "In a world ruled by uncertainty with an uncertain future linked to an actual present, a final position of equilibrium, such as one deals with in static economics, does not properly exist."[31] After all, if the "motive of investors is to accumulate wealth, then a state of rest in the economy is in no sense optimal."[32] Keynes described his own model as a "shifting equilibrium": "Each short-period equilibrium position is temporary. . . . [It] cannot thus be taken to represent a momentary resting place on the road to a long-run period equilibrium."[33]

Investment and Effective Demand

One of Keynes's most important contributions to economic theory was his treatment of investment, for essentially two reasons. First, he stressed the independent nature of investment. In classical and neoclassical theories, investment is constrained by and dependent on the availability of savings in the economy. Keynes, however, saw the operation of a monetary economy with a fully developed banking system as allowing investment to become independent of savings; after all, entrepreneurs can always borrow the necessary funds. Keynes cleared up this "awkward fact" by stating that there is a difference between savings and finance. In an economy with a banking system, there is no reason that firms cannot borrow the necessary credit to invest; thus, there is no need for them to have accumulated savings for initial financing of their investment.

Keynes then went on to argue that investment is the motor of economic growth. Any stringent controls on credit could have detrimental effects on the economy: if investment falls, there will be a recession and unemployment will rise. In this sense, firms' access to finance through commercial banks is crucial.

Investment is also important because it generates income over and above the initial investment. This is what Keynes called the multiplier effect. Through it, investment creates employment and income with which consumers can increase their consumption. In the end, savings will equal investment, because of the income the latter generates. In this sense, savings are dependent on investment, not the reverse. This simple concept is largely misunderstood.

Investment is thus the crucial link in the economy. It can, however, be very volatile, and it is this volatility that explains economic cycles. What, then, governs investment decisions? Unlike neoclassical theory, which argues that the interest rate is a dominant force, Keynes's theory posits that these decisions are ruled by uncertainty about the future and entrepreneurs' expectations of return on investment. Such expectations can change with startling rapidity, which can lead entrepreneurs to postpone or even abandon their investment plans.

The Role of the State

Keynes was interested in the application of theory to the real world. His most important contribution to the area of economic policy is the role he assigned to the state in promoting economic growth. Because he saw capitalism as inherently unstable, Keynes believed that if left to themselves, market forces cannot produce a level of investment sufficient to guarantee the full employment of resources, including labour. Keynes saw a vital role for activist state fiscal policies, but very little use for short-term, quick-fix policies—what many economists have called fine-tuning—which have, unfortunately, come to be associated with him. Despite government policies to this effect, which have dominated most of the post-Second World War era, Keynes saw a more important role for the state, one that implied a long-term view of capital accumulation and investment, which he termed the "socialization of investment." It was one of his most radical ideas, and certainly the least well received by his fellow economists. Since the economy is constrained by the level of effective demand, Keynes believed that under the conditions of a depressed economy, "involuntary unemployment" could be avoided only if the state stimulated one of the components of demand.

The General Theory is a truly remarkable work and a tremendous achievement. Despite certain theoretical errors, "these slips, and various minor criticisms that can be made, do not diminish Keynes's monumental achievement in developing a theory that presents a fundamental challenge to orthodox theory."[34] Although it was written more than fifty-five years ago, the General Theory remains relevant, and reading it is imperative to an understanding modern economies.

In his obituary for Keynes, economist Paul Sweezy noted that the *General Theory* produced a "sense of liberation and intellectual stimulus . . . among younger teachers and students in all the leading British and American universities. . . . Keynes opened up new vistas and new pathways to a whole generation of economists."[35] For some economists and policy makers, these "new vistas" were a threat to capitalism, and many accused Keynes of being a socialist or even of being sympathetic to Marxian economics. In theory and in practice, however, Keynes was strongly opposed to Marxian thought. Perhaps it was because, as a colleague claimed, he "could not make head or tail of Marx";[36] at any rate, Keynes thought that Marx's *Das Kapital* was "out-of-date," academically "controversial-ing" and "unsuitable." Furthermore, he retorted, *Das Kapital's* "contemporary *economic* value . . . is *nil*."[37] Despite describing himself as being on the "extreme left of celestial space," Keynes's objective was not to replace capitalism with socialism—which he saw as outdated—or any other system, but to operate within the existing market system by improving and reforming it.

Keynes believed that the "ideals and policies of socialism [should] adapt to changed historical positions" by abandoning their "doctrinaire slogans of state ownership and class-based revolu-tions."[38] As early as 1923, he remarked that communism had been discredited by events, capitalism had lost its self-confidence, and "socialism in its old-fashioned interpretation, no longer interest[ed] the world."[39]

Was Keynes therefore a socialist, as certain economists claim?[40] The answer is clearly no, if socialism is defined along Marxian variants. However, Keynes did believe in a new, redefined, "prac-tical" socialism—a "particular British socialism, bred out of liberal humanitarianism, big business psychology, and the tradition of public service."[41] His objective was therefore to contribute to a revival of some sort of newly fashioned socialism, which would "motivate and inspire all the constructive temperaments across society, whether in business, labor or elsewhere."[42] By 1939, Keynes had named his vision "liberal socialism,"[43] a blend of individualism and social control.[44]

To those who accused him of sympathizing with Marxists, Keynes simply replied that unmanaged capitalism threatened to destabilize the very foundations of democratic societies. "Whilst, therefore, the enlargement of the functions of government . . . would seem to a nineteenth-century publicist or to a contemporary American financier to be a terrific encroachment on individualism, I defend it, on the contrary, both as the only practicable means of avoiding the destruction of existing economic forms in their entirety and as the condition of the successful functioning of individual initiative."[45]

Keynes did not believe that capitalism seriously misuses or oppresses the different factors of production; however, he felt, it is guilty not of determining the direction of actual employment, but of influencing the volume of unemployment:[46] "The outstanding faults of the economic society in which we live are its failure to provide for full employment and its arbitrary and inequitable distribution of wealth and incomes."[47] Thus, the challenge of economic policy is to reconcile economic efficiency, social justice, and individual liberty. State ownership of the instruments of production was not important for Keynes; the role of the state was to be primarily one of a "guiding influence": "If the State is able to determine the aggregate amount of resources devoted to augmenting the instruments and the basic reward of those who own them, it will have accomplished all that is necessary."[48]

The *General Theory* has not led to the revolution in economic theory that Keynes predicted, for reasons that will be addressed in the next chapter. Despite his claim that his theory was more "general" than neoclassical theory, which he claimed was only a "special case," his confusing and often contradictory comments allowed neoclassical theorists who saw his theory as a threat to reinterpret it as a special case of neoclassical analysis. Attempts to interpret him in this way are simply wrong. His objective was to replace neoclassical theory, not to amend it.

Nonetheless, the *General Theory* still poses a tremendous challenge to orthodox theory and remains a useful starting point for an economic analysis that aims to be relevant to the real world. It is rooted in historical time, in which uncertainty is an important force and social, historical, and institutional arrangements affect economic factors, particularly investment, and it opens up vistas for analysis that are relevant to the operation of actual monetary economies. Keynes addressed many of the issues that I will discuss in this book, and his views, among others', must be considered relevant when discussing unemployment, inflation, and national debt within a contemporary context.

Notes

1. Vicarelli, *Keynes, The Instability*, p. x.
2. Henceforth, Keynes's book will be referred to as the *General Theory*.
3. Keynes, *Collected Writings*, vol. 7, p. 3. Keynes called neoclassical theory "classical."
4. This expression was coined by Adam Smith to mean the free-market system and the self-adjusting nature of capitalism.
5. Keynes, *Collected Writings*, vol. 6, pp. 345–46.
6. Keynes, *Collected Writings*, vol. 7, p. 3.
7. Keynes, *Collected Writings*, vol. 13, p. 492.
8. Ibid., vol. 7, p. v.
9. Asimakopulos, *Keynes's General Theory*, p. xv.
10. Keynes, *Collected Writings*, vol. 13, pp. 469–70.
11. Ibid., vol. 7, pp. v–vi.
12. Ibid., vol. 7, p. viii.
13. Keynes, *Collected Writings*, vol. 14, p. 2, letter to G.F. Shore, 21 Apr. 1936.
14. Kaldor, "Keynesian Economics," p. 3.
15. There will soon be another series of unpublished material by Keynes. *The Collected Philosophical and Other Writings of John Maynard Keynes* will be edited by Rod O'Donnel. See O'Donnel, "The Unwritten Books."
16. Knight, *Risk*, p. 202.
17. In the *General Theory*, Keynes specifically stated, "By 'very uncertain' I do not mean the same thing as 'very improbable.'" Keynes, *Collected Writings*, vol. 7, p. 148, fn1.

18. Keynes, *Collected Writings*, vol. 7, pp. 149–50.
19. Ibid., vol. 14, p. 113. Emphasis added.
20. Weintraub, "Uncertainty," p. 530.
21. Cyert and Simon, "The Behavioral Approach," p. 105.
22. See Lavoie, *Foundations of Post-Keynesian,* pp. 56–7.
23. Ibid., p. 57.
24. Lavoie notes that individuals can either look for alternative actions or abandon or postpone decisions. See Lavoie, *Foundations of Post-Keynesian.*
25. Keynes, *Collected Writings*, vol. 14, p. 115.
26. Carvalho, "On the Concept," p. 265.
27. J. Robinson, *Contribution of Keynes.*
28. Shackle, *Keynesian Kaleidics.*
29. Kaldor, *Economics*, p. 59.
30. Shackle, "Sir John Hicks'," p. 438.
31. Keynes, *Collected Writings*, vol. 19, p. 222.
32. Dow, 1985, p. 127.
33. Asimakopulos, *Keynes's General Theory*, p. 26.
34. Ibid., p. 12.
35. Quoted in Minsky, *John Maynard Keynes*, p. 3.
36. J. Robinson, *History versus Equilibrium.*
37. Keynes, *Collected Writings*, vol. 18, p. 38. This was in a letter addressed to George Bernard Shaw.
38. R. O'Donnel, "The Unwritten Books," p. 782.
39. Keynes, *Collected Writings*, vol. 17, p. 450.
40. See Hymans,*The New Statesman.*
41. Keynes, *Collected Writings*, vol. 20, p. 475.
42. R. O'Donnel, "The Unwritten Books," p. 782.
43. Keynes, *Collected Writings*, vol. 21, p. 500.
44. J. O'Donnel, *Keynes*, ch. 9.
45. Keynes, *Collected Writings,* vol. 7, p. 380.
46. Ibid., vol. 7, p. 379.
47. Ibid., vol. 7, p. 372.
48. Ibid., vol. 7, page 378.

CHAPTER TWO

ECONOMIC ORTHODOXY, OR THE TRIUMPH OF AUSTERITY

Although many economists viewed the impact of Keynes's work, especially the *General Theory*, as revolutionary, for those who were most closely associated with him at Cambridge during that period, the revolution proved "largely aborted."[1] Over the last fifty years, most of Keynes's insights and nuances have been either ignored or incorporated into neoclassical theory, thus leaving "the way economists perceive the world" largely intact.

Neoclassical theory—which one economist called "the valley of darkness"[2]—was developed independently toward the end of the nineteenth century by William Stanley Jevons (1835–82) in England, Carl Menger (1840–1921) in Vienna, and Léon Walras (1834–1910) in France. It represented a clean break from the "classical" theories of Adam Smith, David Ricardo, and Karl Marx, whose explanations of the workings of capitalist economies were strikingly similar.

Smith and Ricardo, writing between 1776 and 1830, at the height of the bourgeois rebellion,[3] did not hesitate to represent society for what it really was (and is): conflicts between various economic and social classes. Marx shared this vision, although there were some differences, of course. For instance, while Ricardo saw the struggle as existing between capitalists and rentiers, Marx saw it as existing between capitalists and workers. It was the latter interpretation that infuriated the ruling class; after all, it is quite normal that in a class society, "the ruling class cannot be indifferent to the type of social science developing in the society in which it holds power."[4] One economist claims, in fact, that "the politically charged direction to Ricardian theory [by Marx] was a factor in the rejection of Ricardo's theory."[5] In other words, "Because Marx's premises were similar to those of the classicals on so many points, it was difficult to reject his analysis his conclusions altogether." The European bourgeoisie therefore rejected classical theory in its entirety, paving the way for a less "class-conscious and more apologetic alternative."[6] With the rise of neoclassical theory, references to class struggle, which was the source of the determination of commodity prices for the classical theorists, disappeared altogether; prices were now determined by supply and demand.

Neoclassical theory has changed very little in the last hundred years, despite the fact that the world, society, and markets have undergone dramatic changes. In fact, it was developed for a particular period in our history (the nineteenth century) that bears little resemblance to today's world, and it could well be argued that it perhaps sufficed to explain economic issues that existed two hundred years ago, but that it has become irrelevant for today's more complex economies. It is in complete disarray; its incapacity to relate theory to the workings of the contemporary world is apparent. Therefore, its predominance may appear puzzling to some. After all, if it has proven to be such a failure, why do economists keep insisting on its validity, and why has it not been replaced with a more realistic theory?

The Dominance of Neoclassical Theory

The reasons are primarily institutional, both within the academic world and in the way society is divided along class lines. In university students' very first encounter with economics, they are introduced to the standard ideas, concepts, and curves that stem from neoclassical theory. They are told that these instruments correspond to how markets actually work: supply and demand determine prices and firms seek to maximize profits. Students do not question this prevalent view, as it corresponds to what they read in newspapers every day. The textbooks offer fascinating and sophisticated proofs, complete with detailed graphs, so students have no reason to question the wisdom of academe. As they continue toward their undergraduate degree, students are taught the same ideas, concepts, and curves, but in greater and more mathematical detail. Preoccupied with obtaining their degree, or fearing a failing grade, they do not oppose neoclassical theory, especially since they are unaware of the existence of alternative theories.

Graduates thus enter the job market having been been fed an exclusive diet of neoclassical theory, and they religiously apply the lessons they have learned. If they decide to pursue advanced studies, the consequences are more alarming. As they pursue master's and doctoral degrees, they are taught the same neoclassical theory, though with an extreme degree of mathematical sophistication. In order to pass their comprehensive exams, they must learn these models. The cycle does not end there; once they obtain their doctorates, many of them return to the university as professors, where they teach the same ideas, concepts, and curves to their students. Others end up working in banks, at large corporations, or as "special advisers" to politicians. Thus, the system is perpetuated.[7]

Professors do not enjoy much more freedom. Tenure is based on quality of publications and the prestige of the journals in which articles are published. Papers that do not deal with trendy topics or use rigorous mathematical neoclassical elements will usually not be accepted for publication in the more respected journals. Heterodox[8] economists often deal with topics outside the interest of neoclassical theory and use vocabulary quite unfamiliar to mainstream economists, who usually control the editorship of journals. As for the content of their courses, until they get tenure, they are more or less bound to teach the mainstream gospel. "From time to time someone is unable any longer to resist the pressure of his doubts and expresses them openly; then, in order, to prevent the scandal spreading, he is promptly silenced, frequently with some concessions and partial admission of his objections, which, *naturally*, the theory had implicitly taken into account."[9]

Pressures to conform to neoclassical theory are being exercised everywhere in the academic world, and the dominance of the orthodox school is easily explained by this phenomenon. But how can we explain the dominance of neoclassical foundations of economic policies? For this, we need to turn to how society is constructed, and who has the most influence over the development of policy. Simply put, the philosophy of neoclassical theory corresponds to the vested interests of the financial and political elites in society, which can more easily influence policy makers and politicians to adopt policies that will benefit them. After all, who else will defend the virtues of free enterprise, no government intervention, and the pursuit of self-interest?

The similarities between neoclassical economics and the objectives of society's elites are overwhelming. The "power struggle" between classes in societies parallels that in economic theory. We must ask who benefits from economic policies based on neoclassical theory. Is it fair to assume that specific classes (or groups) benefit from high interest rates, reductions in corporate taxes, free trade, anti-trust policies, privatization, deregulation, and the minimization of state intervention? As Keynes explained following the triumph of neoclassical theory over classical theory, it did not matter whether the former reaches conclusions different from what the ordinary, uneducated person would expect, or that it could explain and justify social injustice as an inevitable incident in the scheme of natural progress, because it nonetheless afforded a "measure of justification to the free activities of the individual capitalist [and] attracted to it the support of the dominant social force behind authority."[10] It is therefore in the interest of such "individual capitalists" to contribute to the development and assured survival of these sets of ideas. Thus, there is a direct link between the way society and its power relationships are structured and the orientation and development of economic theory, for "any economic system requires a set of rules, an ideology to justify them, and a conscience in the individual which makes him strive to carry them out."[11]

The predominance of neoclassical theory can therefore be explained through the existence of pressures to conform and a power struggle both within and outside of academic institutions. Its survival and proliferation are explained neither through its relevance to the real world nor through its ability to explain market and social phenomena, but through its capacity to generate economic and financial gains to a select few. After all, the poor will never have either the influence or the clout to influence government policy.

Orthodox Neoclassical Theory

It is difficult to disassociate the validity or the essence of a theory from its ideological underpinnings. We must always keep in mind that each paradigm reflects a specific view of the world and how it operates. This view ultimately defines, shapes, and influences policies.

Attempting to define neoclassical theory is a difficult task; some economists find themselves embroiled in long technical essays on its philosophical and ideological elements, while others prefer to define the few elements that form its core, which spans many fields of study and domains of research. The task is further complicated by the lack of consensus on what constitutes pure neoclassical theory. Nonetheless, I will attempt here to summarize the main elements of the theory. Many economists, both orthodox and heterodox, may not agree with my list.[12]

The Individual
The first element setting neoclassical theory apart from other schools of thought is its treatment of the "individual," which is defined as a household or a firm. Individuals, acting independently of one another, play a role in society that is of utmost importance to the functioning of markets. Neoclassical theorists see no useful role for organizations; in fact, society itself is nothing but an extension of individuals, a bottom-up summation of their behaviours; individuals, with their tastes and preferences, constitute the

basic unit upon which neoclassical theory is built. "Individuals are seen as the atoms of society, and no intermediate structure between them and the aggregate society is deemed relevant."[13] As Keynes's contemporary intellectual adversary, Friedrich Hayek, stated, "The first thing that should be said is that [neoclassical theory] is primarily a *theory* of society. . . . There is no other way toward an understanding of social phenomena but through our understanding of individual actions."[14] Individuals' wants and preferences determine the values and the changes in value of all other variables in the economy: the price of goods, the level of wages, and the quantity and type of goods produced.

The objective of all individuals is identical: each seeks to maximize its well-being. In the case of firms, the goal is maximization of profits at all times. It is assumed that markets are governed by purely competitive firms, in which the owner is also the manager; this prevents complications arising from the possibility that owners and managers may not always see eye to eye on various policies.

Households seek to maximize their well-being in their daily exchanges of goods and services. This is called utility—a vague concept defined loosely as satisfaction. It is assumed that households' level of utility is directly related to their consumption of goods; the more they consume, the higher their total utility. They are faced with only one constraint: their income. Households must therefore choose wisely while consuming commodities so as to obtain the best value possible. In other words, they must be efficient.

Individualistic behaviour—what Hayek called true individualism—is believed to lead to the stability of the economy as a whole. This *laissez-faire* philosophy of state minimalism has its theoretical foundations in Adam Smith's *Wealth of Nations*. Smith claimed that by pursuing their own interest, individuals unknowingly promote the over-all welfare of society more effectively than when they actually intend to promote it. The assumption that individuals act according to their own desires and wants, which are related to their personal characteristics rather than to the social, economic, and political environment in which they live has remained largely intact for more than two hundred years.

The problem with the neoclassical assumption of maximization is that it is impossible to specify or observe in the real world. Do firms possess sufficient knowledge of consumers' wants and desires to satisfy them? Do they know how behaviour patterns will change in the future? Not only is this atomistic behaviour impossible to measure, but it also overly simplifies the daily complex, inter-woven behavioural patterns of individuals in society. The real issue is whether there is a plurality of motivations (some of them doubt-less contradictory) or whether self-interest (that is, greed) alone drives human beings.

By making the individual central to their theory, neoclassical economists deliberately exclude from their analysis institutions such as banks, government, and labour unions. They also set aside the impact of social classes, such as capitalists and rentiers, on the economy. The influence of these elements on the overall macro-economic dimension of the markets is believed to be negligible, when they are taken into consideration at all. But individuals are products of their environment—that is, of their "relations with other entities."[15] Any theory must therefore reflect the importance of class pressures and conventions on the decision-making process of both households and firms. Decisions to invest, patterns of con-sumption, and income distribution are causes and results of ongo-ing struggles. Thus, heterodox theorists believe that households are "social beings rather than atomistic ones" and that this "allows . . . for the explicit introduction of dominant institutions and imperfect markets."[16] The limitations of "methodological individualism" are such that the axiomatic construction of society, "starting from agents and the maximizing principle, leads to inextricable situ-ations, which take away from the model any predictive (or even explanatory) content."[17] The economy is not like the solar system or an atom. It is a matter of "human construction and reconstruc-tion. The ideas to which we apply various sets of epistemological criteria or credentials . . . function in the social (re)construction of society."[18]

Rationality

The above discussion of the atomistic behaviour of firms and households ties in well with another important feature of neoclassical theory: rationality. It is not simply the fact that households behave independently from one another that guarantees utility maximization; similarly, competitive firms do not maximize profits simply by being independent. Their rationality guarantees that these objectives will be met. It is assumed, of course, that at all times households and firms make perfectly rational decisions and choose only courses of action that provide maximum satisfaction. In the case of firms, profit maximization would not exist if they were not rational; firms would not know what quantity of goods to produce, and would produce too much or too little. Neoclassical theory further assumes that all agents possess the same information and react the same way. This allows actions to be predicted, and eliminates any unforeseen events.

Rationality, or "substantive rationality," is a powerful assumption, resting on a Cartesian approach to human behaviour. In every situation, neoclassical theory has faith that individuals will always do what is expected of them.

The notion of rationality is not, however, accepted by all economists. Many argue that it undermines the roles of institutions in society and their importance in and influence on decision making. Rationality fails to take into account the human condition, the length of experience, the need to act, and the vagueness of knowledge and information. This is not to say that economic agents are totally irrational; however, individuals are limited in what they can do not just by income, but by a variety of other constraints. Even if they had perfect information, they would still be constrained by their ability and capacity to act, and by time. In this sense, rationality is of a "procedural" nature, and is often referred to as "bounded" rationality. A specialist in this area of research noted the difference between the two interpretations of rationality: "Behavior is substantively rational when it is appropriate to the achievement of goals within the limits imposed by given conditions and constraints. . . . Given these goals, the rational behavior is determined entirely by the characteristics of the environment in which it takes place. . . . Behavior is procedurally rational when it is the outcome of appropriate deliberation."[19]

Individuals face not only external constraints, such as the quantity of information available at any given point in time, but also internal constraints or limitations, which may compromise their ability always to choose the "best" solution—that is, utility or profit maximization. "The rationality of the business firm is a rationality that takes account of the limits on its knowledge, on its information, on its capacity for computation, and on its understanding of theory. It is a rationality that makes intensive use of rules of thumb where a more exact application of theory is impossible whether because the theory is not understood, because the data needed for estimating its parameters is not available, or because the decision must be made under conditions of uncertainty."[20]

Rules of thumb, as noted above, play an important part in the behaviour and decision making of procedurally rational individuals. Households and firms often rely on past decisions and decisions of their peers when choosing between various possible scenarios. Furthermore, they may not always choose the right course of action, because there is too little—or too much—information. Behaviour contains an element of uncertainty that plays hob both with social processes and with the accuracy of their representation in mathematical models. When it departs from the pattern of expectations on which an economic theory is based, the relevance of that theory becomes blurred.

Markets and the Forces of Supply and Demand
Analysis of supply and demand is not an exclusive feature of neoclassical theory, since even heterodox economists make use of these concepts. However, orthodox economists have a special faith

in these curves, and their approach to and interpretation of the interaction between the two concepts are an aspect unique to neoclassical theory.

The supply and demand curves of a particular commodity, within the context of neoclassical theory, are believed to be "well behaved": they answer the basic nature of human behaviour. The relationship between price and quantity demanded and those supplied are thus based on rationality. For consumers, it is rational to assume that when prices decrease, consumption increases. The inverse is true for firms: when prices rise, a firm will be encouraged to increase production because its revenues will increase as well. It is this inverse relationship that guarantees the stability of markets. The Smithian "invisible hand" will direct market forces to the point where quantity supplied and quantity demanded will be equal at a given price. When prices are too low, consumers will want to increase their consumption, while firms will be encouraged to produce less. However, since there will be an excess demand for goods, prices will be pushed up, reducing consumption and increasing production. This process will continue until supply equals demand and the market is cleared. Thus, prices are a market-clearing mechanism.

The interaction of the curves determines, within each market, the price and the quantity to be produced. Prices will adjust upward or downward in order to guarantee market clearing. Thus, prices are flexible. Any failure of markets to clear is blamed entirely on price rigidities, or the existence of other types of market "imperfections," such as monopolies, oligopolies, governments, and unions. Otherwise, markets guarantee an "efficient" allocation of raw materials among sectors in the economy, and full employment is achieved. The belief in a free-enterprise system and its capacity to generate full employment and prosperity is grounded in the neoclassical economic law established by French economist Jean-Baptiste Say in 1803, which says that products (commodities) always exchange for products—or, as James Mill put it in 1808, "Supply creates its own demand." This law implies that there can never be an economic downturn or a recession (a "generalized glut") since production always creates sufficient income to guarantee clearing of markets at a given price. Similarly, there can never be unemployment.

There is, however, much to criticize in these two basic tenets of neoclassical economic theory. When uncertainty is introduced, it becomes impossible to predict how consumers and sellers will react given changes in prices. There is no guarantee that the supply and demand curves will be well behaved. For instance, with uncertainty regarding the future, consumers may react to a rise in price by increasing their purchases in anticipation of further price increases. Similarly, sellers may decide to reduce their offer in the hope that prices will continue to rise. Therefore, it is impossible to determine any equilibrium position, because we never know, from one moment to the next, where the curves will settle or even what they look like.

The Exchange Economy

Neoclassical theory has it that strong self-adjusting mechanisms will ensure that markets are always operating at full employment. If there is a surplus or a shortage in certain markets, the "invisible hand" will ensure that resources are redirected instantaneously,[21] through market forces, to compensate for any imperfections—a simple exchange of raw materials and other resources, such as labour, between different markets.

Since the economy always functions at full employment, the notion of scarcity is also paramount to neoclassical theory. Resources are considered scarce, so their proper and efficient distribution among markets is important in order to achieve maximum output (again the notion of maximization). Since there are decisions to be made regarding where resources are to be funneled through market forces, the notion of opportunity cost becomes important as well. The relative scarcity of goods is reflected in prices: the rarer the good, the higher its price. This would explain the price differential between diamonds, coal, and potato chips.

As goods become rare, supply is reduced, raising prices. Furthermore, "when all resources are scarce, they are fully employed, and therefore all questions revolve around the proper use of *existing* resources, rather than the creation of new resources."[22]

The notion of scarcity is tied to that of exchange. In neoclassical theory, markets are analyzed as if commodities were not produced, as if everything simply existed. Individuals are said to have "endowments," which they exchange with others. This concept is one of indirect exchange; workers exchange their labour services for commodities produced. It is assumed that endowments are fixed, and that they cannot be increased. "This meant that an 'economy' . . . was necessarily constrained in its activism by its resource endowment: it was the poverty (or insufficiency) of resources which limited the satisfaction of wants. . . . The welfare of the community would be maximized only by the free play of market forces under a free enterprise system, with the minimum of government interference and regulation."[23]

Contrary to the neoclassical emphasis on exchange and scarcity, heterodox economists have stressed the capacity of economies to reproduce.[24] The emphasis is thus shifted to accumulation and economic growth. Scarcity makes little sense in economies in which firms generally produce well under full capacity, with an obvious underutilization of the factors of production—labour, in particular. The chief constraint is therefore not scarcity, but effective demand. This is in stark contrast to neoclassical theory: "Scarcity is the essence of neoclassical economics. To proclaim the existence of an economy of plenty is to negate the foundations of orthodoxy."[25]

Equilibrium

In neoclassical theory, everything is viewed from a perspective of equilibrium in the position of the economy and of economic variables over the long run. The economy is said to be in equilibrium when there is no tendency for it to move away from its position. For example, once the economy is at full employment, there is obviously little incentive for markets to change. In this situation, markets are said to be in long-run equilibrium, since only then are resources being used efficiently. Market forces act to push the economy toward this final resting position, which is also referred to as Walrasian equilibrium, as it is rooted in the work of nineteenth-century French economist Léon Walras, who developed the first mathematical version of neoclassical theory. Any other situation, such as a position in which there is unemployment or inflation, is seen as disequilibrium.

Neoclassical theory assumes that, due to market forces and the "invisible hand," there is a "natural" tendency for markets to gravitate toward long-run equilibrium, which is the only logical position. Indeed, within the context of the theory, flexible prices, atomistic maximizing behaviour, and rationality all guarantee long-run equilibrium.

The concept of long-run equilibrium, coupled with sophisticated models, allows economists to explore the growth path of the economy over time. The trouble with this analysis is that it does not take into account the social and structural changes generated by the passage of time. How can certain variables be allowed to remain fixed while others are allowed to change?

Models and Mathematics

The importance of models in economics cannot be overstated. It is virtually impossible to define, describe, or explain a theory without falling back on some sort of graph, curve, or mathematical equation. However, economists must be skeptical of models; there is much they can tell us, but only when they are well used; blind reliance on them to justify the validity of a theory can prove to be an Achilles' heel. Models are always based on a series of assumptions that are meant to describe a theory; these assumptions are the delimitations of the theory and must be scrutinized along with it. If the assumptions of the model are not sound, neither is the theory. In a letter to a colleague, Keynes was clear on this issue: "One cannot get very far except by devising new and improved models. This requires, as you say, 'a vigilant observation of the actual workings of our system.'"[26] As Keynes also noted, economics "is a science of thinking in terms of models joined to the art of choosing models which are relevant to the contemporary world. . . . Good economists are scarce because the gift for using 'vigilant observations' to choose good models, although it does not require a highly specialized intellectual technique, appears to be a very rare one."[27]

Economists state that models must be a simplification of reality, which is far too complex and has too many highly interdependent variables for models to capture all of its intricacies. There is no argument on this issue, as all economists aim to simplify; what is hotly debated is precisely what is to be left out. "Knowing how to simplify one's description of reality without neglecting anything essential is the most important part of the economist's art."[28] However, the economist is "subject to a strong temptation either to include in his list assumptions which bring the problem close to the real problems, but which make it quite insoluble by the technique at his command, or to confine the problem within the limits which make it soluble but to hide the assumptions which bound it (if he is too honest to omit them altogether) in a dusty corner of the footnote where he hopes that no one will notice them."[29]

Heterodox theorists believe that economists must start their research from observations, from which they work out a consistent and logical theory. A model must ask pertinent questions. It should make the real world intelligible, and not explain how it would operate if it were rid of uncertainty, government intervention, monopolies, unions, and banks. Clearly, it should not "substitute an ideal theoretical world remote from the facts of experience in order to make the analysis easily tractable."[30]

Neoclassical theorists do not agree. They believe that the lack of realism underlying the fundamental assumptions of a model is not important and have a tendency to choose axioms or assumptions "not for their likelihood, but for their ability to allow the existence of an equilibrium or its uniqueness. [They] describe the world as it *should* be rather than as *it is*. If they reinforce the ideal of long-run equilibrium, no matter how abstract or how removed they are from reality, then they are valid."[31] Many heterodox economists place the emphasis on explaining markets, rather than on predicting their behaviour. "The new vision is concerned with seeing how an economy keeps going [accumulation], what is *supposed* to happen, but that to discover what makes it break down and what makes it develop into an economy of a different kind."[32] Thus, we must ask, given that neoclassical theory does not deal with uncertainty, whether its assumptions of rationality, utility and profit maximization, and long-run equilibrium, and the neoconservative policies based on them, are realistic and useful.

Mathematics and statistics hold a particular place in economic theory, since they are usually used to demonstrate the validity of a theory. It is characteristic of neoclassical theorists to ignore the effects of statistical facts upon their conclusions. (Statistics can be inaccurate or misinterpreted, and therefore should be used with caution.) In neoclassical theory in particular, the validity of any assumption is based on the notion of optimization—the ability to hold up to mathematical scrutiny. In this context, profit or utility maximization, long-run equilibrium, efficiency, scarcity, prices, and rationality are all reduced to mathematical equations, and so is human behaviour. A household will be rational only if mathematically its behaviour can lead to an observable level of utility maximization. This logic may be strong, but its assumptions are not an accurate representation of the real world.

According to Milton Friedman, the only valid test of a model is whether it provides the tools to predict future outcomes accurately, and these predictions are relevant only when they deal with long-run equilibrium values of variables such as price level, unemployment, and economic growth. A theory must abstract from the

mass of complex and detailed circumstances as surrounding the phenomena to be explained. . . . To be important a hypothesis must be descriptively false in its assumptions. . . . The relevant question to ask about the "assumptions" of a theory is not whether they are descriptively "realistic," for they never are, but whether they are sufficiently good approximation for the purpose at hand. And this question can be answered only by seeing whether the theory works, which means it yields sufficiently accurate predictions. . . . The ultimate goal of a positive science is the development of a "theory" or "hypothesis" that yields valid and meaningful . . . predictions about phenomena not yet observed.[33]

But how can we realistically predict events? As an econometrician once noted, econometrics—the use of sophisticated statistical models—cannot lead to an objective, positive science of economics because statistical inference depends on human opinion, judgment, and conviction: "Economists have inherited from the physical sciences the myth that scientific inference is objective and free of prejudice."[34]

In neoclassical theory, mathematical expressions are retained primarily for aggregative analysis, not for their ability to explain real-world events or individual and collective behaviour. There is, however, a definite trade-off between mathematics and reality: "The careful accumulation and sifting of statistics and the development of refined methods of statistical inference cannot make up for the lack of any basic understanding of how the actual economy works."[35] In most cases, they are not appropriate to the problems at hand.

In the orthodox context, economics is reduced to a pure science like physics, and the economy is thought to be ruled by a set of exclusive, immutable laws, similar to those in a controlled physics experiment, leaving no possibility for unexpected events. The only remaining purpose of economic research is to estimate the parameters and predict the future. Neoclassical theory is thus static in the sense that all parameters of economic behaviour are fixed.

Blind reliance on mathematics is questionable, however, especially in a discipline like economics. The belief in a calculable future in which statistical laws of probability are used to forecast events seriously underestimates the role and importance of human error and uncertainty. Or, as one economist has put it, "On the one hand is the good news: the intuitions of Adam Smith and many later writers can indeed be rigorously formulated and proved. The bad news is that the theorem depends on a host of conditions, many of dubious realism."[36]

The only real use for complicated mathematical formulas is to give economics the appearance of a truly rigorous science:

> [Many] of the ablest minds attracted into professional economics find their exposure to general equilibrium theory the most exciting intellectual experience of their lives. Elegant, rigorous, mathematically powerful, the theory . . . gives economics a theoretical core that "softer" social sciences lack and often envy. It "is the only game in town." It especially enchants those who were drawn into the profession *more because it challenges their mathematical and logical skills* than because it might help to solve real world puzzles and problems. . . . The potent and admitted unrealism of assumptions does not matter.[37]

Thus, the debate over the scientific nature of economics is simply a smoke screen; it allows economists the luxury of ignoring the notion of uncertainty. And, as was observed by one neoclassical theorist, uncertainty renders neoclassical theory obsolete.

The presence of uncertainty makes it impossible for economics to be considered "hard" science. There are no constants in economics comparable to the law of gravity in physics. Parameters and their values change, just as the real world is a continually evolving and unpredictable place. There is no way of knowing the value of unemployment, prices, wages, level of investment, aggregate demand, and savings one year into the future, let alone five or ten years hence; economic forecasts regarding the growth of the economy only months ahead are constantly being revised to take into account changing values of certain parameters. In fact, economics is "on the edge of science and the edge of history"[38]—or, as Keynes put it, "Economics is essentially a moral science and not a natural one."[39] It is in response to this blind reliance on mathematics that economist Joan Robinson was said to have commented that she never learned mathematics to develop theory, so she had to learn to *think* about problems.

This is not to say that economists should never use mathematics, statistics, or models, but that they must be aware of their limitations. Keynes was not against the use of mathematics in economics, as long as it was a means, not an end in itself. His goal was not to deny all validity to formal methods; rather, it was to understand and appreciate the "limitations arising out of the inescapable vagueness of human knowledge about economic processes which are uncertain, complex and organic in nature."[40] Keynes believed that the illegitimate use of mathematics in economics would lead to the following conclusions:[41] a divorce between analysis and reality;[42] a divorce between analysis and common sense;[43] it can give the economist a false aesthetic satisfaction;[44] it can lead the economist to concentrate on mathematics for its own sake and to abandon any link with economics;[45] and it can lead to a loss of substance and meaning.[46]

In neoclassical theory, assumptions are chosen exclusively for their amenability to mathematical manipulation rather than for their relevance to the real world. As one econometrician noted, a "mathematical or logical proof of internal consistency offers merely a deductive demonstration that the proper *a priori* assumptions have been made and that credible rules have been followed to reach desirable or correct results. . . . But the demonstration *does not* prove that the argument corresponds to the real world one is ostensibly explaining."[47] Deductive logic only makes models tautological. In the *General Theory*, Keynes stated that

> the object of our analysis is not to provide a machine, or method of blind manipulation, which will furnish an infallible answer, but to provide ourselves with an organized and orderly method of thinking out particular problems; and, after we have reached a provisional

conclusion by isolating the complicating factors one by one, we then have to go back on ourselves and allow, as well as we can, for the probable interactions of the factors amongst themselves. This is the nature of economic thinking. Any other way of applying our formal principles of thought . . . will lead us into error. [Furthermore, it is] a great fault of symbolic pseudo-mathematical methods of formalizing a system of economic analysis . . . that they expressly assume strict independence between the factors involved and lose their cogency and authority if this hypothesis is disallowed. . . . Too large a proportion of recent "mathematical" economics are mere concoctions, as imprecise as the initial assumptions they rest on, which allow the author to lose sight of the complexities and interdependence of the real world in a maze of pretentious and unhelpful symbols.[48]

In this opinion, Keynes was following in the footsteps of his mentor, Alfred Marshall, who, having taught mathematics at St. John's College before switching to economics, came to realize the limitations of applying mathematical models to economics: "I had a growing feeling in the later years of my work that a good mathematical theorem dealing with economic hypotheses was very unlikely to be good economics."[49]

The increasing use of sophisticated mathematics in economics has led some to refer to it as an "inward" science. Referring to neoclassical theory and the parallel use of statistical models, it can be argued that

having accomplished much it turned inward, developing more elaborated and sophisticated techniques rather than attempting to expand the analysis to include the more important developments in the evolution of capitalism. The result has been that the technical success of neoclassical analysis has been purchased at a great cost, that of simplifying to such a degree that the approach has very limited explanatory power.[50]

The "Keynesian" Experience

The *General Theory* generated a vast body of literature, as well as policy initiatives after the Second World War, that were labeled "Keynesian," primarily because governments adopted massive expansionary fiscal policies. Did these policies find theoretical support in Keynes? Is Keynesian economics the same as the "economics of Keynes"?[51]

Most individuals and almost all economists firmly believe that Canada and most developed countries followed and adopted policies that found theoretical support in Keynes's work. If this were true, we could draw two important conclusions. First, Keynes's premonitions came true, a revolution did take place; second, judging by the rise of anti-Keynesian neoconservative economic policies since the mid-1970s, Keynes's revolution was a failure.

The questions must therefore be asked, Was there truly a Keynesian "revolution"? Was there indeed a period in our history in which governments adopted the policies of Keynes? Were neoclassical theory and philosophy ever rejected? The answer to all of them is simple, yet perhaps surprising: no. Despite all the rhetoric to the contrary, the policies adopted were not entirely representative of the ideas of Keynes, and were in fact closer to those defended by mainstream economists. Thus, "in the area of fiscal policy Keynes's proposals could not be judged to have failed for the simple reason that they have never been implemented."[52]

If this is so, how then can we account for this myth? To comprehend what is involved, we must understand the historical context within which the *General Theory* was written, and how the ideas were developed.

The *General Theory* was developed in the Cambridge oral tradition, following discussions Keynes had with his fellow economists on earlier drafts of his book. The Circus, as the members of this group called it, included such prominent economists as Richard Khan, James Meade, Joan and Austin Robinson, and Piero

Sraffa. While the *General Theory* dealt with issues that were of particular interest to the members of the Circus, economists outside the group did not have the privilege of those discussions. When the *General Theory* was published, the ideas and vocabulary, though clear to Keynes's colleagues, were foreign to most economists who had studied neoclassical theory, leaving them open to misanalysis and misinterpretation.

In the United States, a group of younger economists, some of whom went on to become Nobel Prize laureates, were also unconvinced of the strength and validity of neoclassical theory and policies. By then, the American economy was deteriorating badly, and capitalism was threatened. New policies, new ideas, and, most of all, a new philosophy were needed. Many of these economists were eager to break away from the hold of orthodox theory, despite having been nurtured on it. The *General Theory* seemed to be a much-needed breakthrough, and they quickly championed the policies they thought were described in the book.

The *General Theory* was, however, difficult to read, and its unconventional concepts were not easy to understand. The American economists were unable to appreciate completely Keynes's outright and sometimes vicious rejection of neoclassical theory and his "revolutionary" ideas. They did not understand his analytical structure, and "they did not wish entirely to destroy the analytical structure which they had spent years in school learning to master. They therefore tried to amalgamate the neoclassical theoretical analysis with Keynes's activist policies."[53]

Keynes's very limited use of mathematics also proved to be unfamiliar to these economists, who were accustomed to judging an economic model on the rigour of its mathematical implications. In this sense, Keynes's writing was said to be more "feminine rather than precise, ordered, and meticulous."[54] This view was expressed more clearly many years later: "Keynes did not help [American economists] understand his point. In keeping from the ethnocentrism of English economics, especially at Cambridge, he paid little attention to continental writers. . . . Keynes used simple mathematics, and that sparingly. His language, his terminology, and style of argument were pragmatic and worldly like Alfred Marshall's rather than rigorous and abstract like Walras's."[55]

Having misunderstood Keynes, American economists then went on to formulate policies that were only partly based on ideas found in the *General Theory*. The most important and revolutionary aspects, such as the notions of historical time, uncertainty, and production, were omitted from "Keynesian" policies, which the American economists called "neoclassical synthesis Keynesianism." Thus, neoclassical theory survived, slightly altered, and the Keynesian "revolution" never took place:

> The doctrines of the new era have been attributed to Keynes, but the dominant economic theory of the time in North America and spreading from there over the world, is what I have called the "Bastard Keynesian doctrine." I do not use this term just as abuse. It has a definite meaning. . . . The Bastard Keynesian doctrine allowed all the old doctrine to creep back in again. Keynes was diagnosing a defect inherent in capitalism. But the Bastard Keynesians turned the argument back into a defense of laissez-faire. The old orthodoxy of laissez-faire, against which the Keynesian Revolution was raised, taught that the free play of free market forces could be relied upon to establish equilibrium with full employment.[56]

It was a return to a pre-Keynesian world of self-adjusting markets.

Other economists arrived at the same conclusions: "It is a matter of significance therefore that Keynes cannot be claimed by any school of Keynesians, if only because his method of economic analysis was central and unique. Keynes's philosophy was not formulated along the lines of natural science, but in terms of an old duality, of practical wisdom based on ideals, versus the transience of the world."[57] Furthermore, "Revolutions have a nasty way of devouring their progenitors and replacing them by a lesser and more arrogant breed who, in the name of the revolution, seek to consolidate its gain only to betray it in the process."[58]

One of the most striking examples is Keynes's treatment of equilibrium. As explained above, Keynes rejected the notion that the economy was, at any given point in time, moving "naturally" toward a position of long-run equilibrium. His intellectual efforts were directed toward convincing his fellow economists that the real world is so fraught with uncertainty that long-run equilibrium can be considered only one resting position among many others. He also accused neoclassical economists of not being able to define this long-run period: was it ten years, twenty years, or even longer? As he put it, "This long-run is a misleading guide to current affairs. In the long-run we are all dead. Economists set themselves too easy, too useless a task if in tempestuous seasons they can only tell us that when the storm is long past, the ocean is flat again."[59]

This simple idea was, however, lost in the American version of Keynes's theories. In fact, although "bastard Keynesians" recognized that markets could, in the short run, be stuck in a position of less than full employment, they thought that the economy could eventually attain long-run equilibrium; it might simply take too long to make the necessary adjustments, due to market "imperfections." They believed that when Keynes made a case for more government involvement in the economy, this meant that short-run lapses from full employment could be offset by means of government policy—that governments could provide "quick-fix" policies that would shock the economy back to long-run equilibrium, where neoclassical theory "would come into its own again." Active counter-cyclical policies were needed to keep the economy as close to full employment as possible. As we shall see, Keynes was essentially against such policy initiatives, and against the use of government funds to "boost" the economy. Nonetheless, this view became the the cornerstone of government policy in North America during the 1950s and 1960s. "Bastard Keynesianism" simply became a "kinder and gentler" version of neoclassical theory.

One of the first interpretations of the *General Theory* was offered by Sir John Hicks, who developed a mathematical model believed to be based on the works of Walras. This approach could also, according to Hicks, incorporate four key elements of Keynes's analysis—investments, savings, liquidity demand, and money supply—and has come to be known as the IS-LM model. American "Keynesians" quickly seized on the concept and used it as the foundation of their own version of Keynesianism.

Hicks, however, grew increasingly dissatisfied with his IS-LM model. Although he won the 1972 Nobel Prize in economics for it, he wrote in 1977 that it "was done a long time ago, and it was with mixed feelings that I found myself honoured for that work, which I felt myself to have outgrown. The time came when I felt that I had done with it. . . . I could see that it was nonsense. It does deliberate violence to the *order* in which the real world . . . events occur."[60] A few years after that, Hicks claimed he had "become dissatisfied with it."[61]

With Hicks's rejection of his own work—a rejection that economists still ignore—it should be clear that the "Keynesian" experience was not based on ideas put forward by Keynes. Since this is the case, and given the current failure of neoclassical fiscal and monetary policies to deal with unemployment, the debt, and other economic problems, there is perhaps a great need to go back to Keynes's writings. Of course, the world has changed a great deal since 1936, and some of Keynes's ideas may not be completely appropriate or applicable. However, many are still relevant to the workings of our economy and the real world, and the rest can certainly be adapted to take into consideration the changing world order. The inherent uncertainty of markets is still with us, and Keynes provided a serious blueprint of how to deal with an unknown future. Most of all, he showed that uncertainty governs economic cycles, and economic policies should therefore take it into account.

In the 1970s, with the OPEC oil crisis, "Keynesian" policies hit a snag when modern economies witnessed simultaneous high unemployment and inflation, always thought to be an impossible occurrence. Since "Keynesian" theory failed to explain or provide suitable and workable solutions to the inflation problem, it was quickly abandoned and full-blown neoclassical theory was reinstated.

The remainder of this book will concentrate on three major economic issues: the debt, inflation, and unemployment. In each chapter, the neoclassical approach will be discussed, and then rejected for its lack of realism. An alternative approach will be presented, based on the writings of Keynes and faithful post-Keynesians. I do not claim that these are the only solutions to our many problems; but if decision makers were to make use of Keynes's philosophy and approach to economics, they would have access to policy advice that reflects the "facts of experience" and the workings of the real-world economy, rather than that of a hypothetical, utopian world.

Notes

1. Eichner and Kregel, "Essay in Post-Keynesian Theory," p. 1293.
2. Eichner, *The Macrodynamics*, p. 1.
3. Sherman, "The Sad State."
4. DeVroey, "The Transition," p. 416.
5. Dow, 1985, p. 50.
6. Lavoie, *Foundations of Post-Keynesian*, p. 18.
7. J. Robinson, *Collected Economic Papers*, p. 127.
8. The word "heterodox" is used to define economists who oppose neoclassical (orthodox) economic theory. While post-Keynesians are the dominant group, other heterodox groups include neo-Ricardians and institutionalists.
9. Sraffa, "Laws of Return," p. 536.
10. Keynes, *Collected Writings*, vol. 7, p. 33.
11. J. Robinson, *Economic Philosophy*, p. 13.
12. For this summary, I drew on Marc Lavoie's classification. See Lavoie, "Towards a New Research Programme."
13. DeVroey, "The Transition," p. 416.
14. Hayek, *Individualism and Economic Order*, p. 6.
15. Winslow, "Organic Interdependence," p. 1173.
16. Lavoie, *Foundations of Post-Keynesian*, p. 11.
17. Guerrien, *Concurrence, flexibilité et stabilité*, p. 290.
18. Samuels, "Truth and Discourse," p. 518.
19. Simon, "From Substantive," pp. 130–1.
20. Cyert and Simon, "The Behavioral Approach," p. 104.
21. Paul Davidson compares this concept to the Big Bang theory of creation, in which everything is determined at once. See Davidson, *Controversies*.

22. Lavoie, *Foundations of Post-Keynesian*, p. 45.
23. Kaldor, "Keynesian Economics After Fifty Years," pp. 1–2.
24. See Roncaglia, *Sraffa*, p. 5.
25. Lavoie, *Foundations of Post-Keynesian*, p. 14.
26. Keynes, *Collected Writings*, vol. 14, letter to Ray Harrod, p. 296.
27. Quoted in Harrod, "Note on A Treatise," p. 256.
28. Duesenberry, *Business Cycles*, pp. 14–15.
29. J. Robinson, *Economics of Imperfect Competition*, p. 2.
30. Davidson, *Controversies in Post Keynesian Economics*, p. 30.
31. Lavoie, "Towards a New Research Programme," p. 42. Emphasis added.
32. Nell, "The Revival," p. 8.
33. M. Friedman, *Essays in Positive Economics*, p. 23.
34. Leimer, "Let's Take the Con," p. 36.
35. Kaldor, "The Irrelevance," p. 1240.
36. Tobin, "Theoretical Issues," p. 110. Emphasis added.
37. Ibid., p. 115. Emphasis added.
38. Hicks, *Causality in Economics*, p. 38.
39. Keynes, *Collected Writings*, vol. 14, p. 297. Letter to R.F. Harrod, 1938.
40. Gerrard, "Human Logic in Keynes's Thought."
41. See J. O'Donnel, *Keynes*, pp. 189–90.
42. Keynes, *Collected Writings*, vol. 7, p. 298, 280 fn.
43. Ibid., vol. 8, p. 424.
44. Ibid., vol. 14, pp. 511–12.
45. Ibid., vol. 11, p. 195.
46. Ibid., vol. 29, p. 38.
47. Henry, "On Equilibrium," p. 217.
48. Keynes, *Collected Writings*, vol. 7, pp. 297–8.
49. Marshall, *Principles of Economics*, 9th ed., p. 775. Letter to A.L. Bowley, 27 Feb. 1906.
50. Cornwall, *Conditions*, p. 14.
51. Peterson, "Institutionalism," p. 3.
52. Kregel, "Monetary Production Economics," p. 221.
53. Davidson, *Controversies in Post Keynesian Economics*, p. 15.
54. A. Robinson, "Could There Have Been," p. 90.
55. Tobin, "Theoretical Issues in Macroeconomics," p. 110.
56. J. Robinson, *Collected Economic Papers*, vol. 5, p. 121.
57. Fitzgibbons, "From Keynes's Vision," p. 20.
58. Rousseas, *Post Keynesian Monetary Economics*, p. 3.
59. Keynes, *Collected Writings*, vol. 13, p. 492.
60. Hicks, *Economic Perspectives*, pp. v–vi.
61. Hicks, "ISLM—An Explanation," p. 139.

CHAPTER THREE

THE DEBT AND THE POLITICS OF AUSTERITY

There is no economic issue in Canada today receiving as much attention as our "enormous" debt.[1] We need only to pick up a copy of any daily newspaper or listen ever so faintly to what our politicians are saying to realize that the debt is *the* burning policy issue, the centre around which everything else seems to revolve. Many politicians would like to see legislated balanced budgets; others, less radical, categorically state that debt is at an unacceptable level and must be reduced at once, though they do not specify by how much. We are reminded time and time again of the dire consequences we face unless we somehow reduce—or even eliminate—our debt. We are told how it cripples our economy, threatens our way of life and standard of living and those of our children, and prevents us from achieving our social and economic objectives. We are also reminded that Canada is not the only nation to be "cursed" with the dreadful burden of debt. From country to country, anti-debt policies are remarkably the same: raising taxes and cutting back indiscriminately on government spending. Fighting the debt has become the cornerstone of mainstream economic thinkers and policy analysts.

The consensus that has formed around the question of the debt is, however, not complete. On the one hand, mainstream economists adopt a Hayekian neoconservative view that the debt and deficits are necessarily evil and at the root of our ailing economies; therefore, drastic debt reduction must be a priority of all governments, and the consequences of this action pale in comparison to those awaiting us if we do not act immediately. Even if these consequences are greater unemployment in the short and long runs or a massive deficit in our social infrastructure, this is somehow a fair price to pay, since, in the end, markets—and hence consumers—will automatically be better off.

On the other hand, heterodox economists believe that the consequences of massive debt reduction are far worse than the mainstream economists claim and that they would end up destabilizing the economy for years—if not generations—to come. In fact, if used properly, they believe, debt can become the engine of economic growth and prosperity. As economist Mario Seccareccia stated recently in *The Canadian Forum* (June 1993, p. 9), "The first question we should ask is . . . Can we have growth in the economy without debt? The answer, I am sure, is going to be 'No', we cannot."

It should be noted that there is a fundamental double standard when it comes to comparing public and private debt. Whereas public debt is thought to be wasteful and inefficient, there is the perception that private debt is acceptable. This argument is weak; debt by any other name is still debt. No one doubts for an instant that private-sector firms must get into debt if they want to start or expand business activities. Debt is *their* engine of growth. In fact, our entire economy is built on the understanding that, if used properly, private debt creates revenues and employment. In comparing public and private debt, we find some startling figures. The growth of private debt in Canada has averaged 14 per cent a year since 1980, while public debt has grown by only 6 per cent over the same period.[2] As well, private-sector debt has primarily been used, especially in recent years, to finance unproductive and largely inefficient investments, such as mergers, take-overs, and speculation in commercial real estate. These investments add nothing to capital accumulation and contribute very little to the economy or to economic growth.

Neoclassical economists' opposition to debt must be construed as a fundamental opposition to government or state intervention, which debt ultimately represents. This is not an economic argument, but a political and ideological one. Since their theory is based on the primacy of the individual and of market forces, they cannot recognize the benefits of government debt.

Indeed, the debate in Canada concerning government or state intervention is no longer based on *how* governments can help society achieve full employment, stimulate the economy, or increase standards of living. These issues, and many more, dominated the postwar period up to the late 1970s, when the conventional wisdom was that government had a legitimate reason, on behalf of the greater community, to intervene in the economy in order to rectify weaknesses inherent to the capitalist system. In essence, many perceived government intervention as instrumental in achieving a higher standard of living for all Canadians. However, with the rise of neoconservatism in Canada and around the world (which occurred at the same time as the rise in inflation—not a coincidence, as we shall see below), the tone of the debate quickly changed. Suddenly, there no longer appeared to be an appropriate role for governments in the marketplace. Market forces and the "invisible hand" became the only accepted dogma; in the course of only a few years, the debate shifted back fifty years to a pre-Keynesian era. Governments were seen as inefficient and an obstacle to growth. "Savage" capitalism was believed to be the best (read, *only*) way to achieve full employment and an "efficient"—although not necessarily equitable—income distribution. There can be no doubt that the current fight against deficits and debt is an ideologically driven attack on the state.

While economists are clearly divided on the issue, the demarcations are more nebulous when it comes to politics and political parties. If the political right has traditionally been the driving force behind a *laissez-faire* approach to economics based on individualism and state minimalism, the political left has also accepted somewhat this anti-Keynesian perspective on the economy. We need only look at the economic policies of provincial NDP governments in Canada to see that the left has caved in and espoused the same economic anti-debt rhetoric as the right. Even the vocabulary is the same; they speak of "fiscal responsibility" and of the "new realities." If this is the case, then, as columnist Rick Salutin pointed out in *Saturday Night* (May 1993, p. 19), why should we even bother having a left in Canada? "Unless you challenge neoconservative rhetoric and that basic world view," Salutin argues, "then even when the right loses, they sort of win because they've set the ground rules and everyone else has accepted them." This view was shared by columnist Charles Gordon, who recently stated (*Maclean's,* 22 Feb. 1993, p. 11), "If it were only Conservatives who were affected by the messages they put out in the 1980s, the answer would be simple: throw out the Conservatives and never let them in again. But all parties have been affected. They are frightened and demoralized, afraid to act. The notion of the deficit, an economic monster movie created and directed by Reaganites, Thatcherites and Mulroneyites, has troubled the sleeping and waking hours of even Liberals and New Democrats." It becomes a vicious circle: with public opinion hardening, politicians do not dare to speak of the positive aspects of debt or the true causes of the current debt in a rational and honest way. Afraid of being ridiculed, they choose to retreat into their comfortable plotting rooms and accept the myths, fiddling while Canada burns. The consequence of all this muddling has been for some postmodern intellectuals officially to declare the end of ideologies—that in fact, there is no longer, and perhaps never has been, such a thing as "left" and "right."[3]

Canadians must realize that, if used properly, debt can be an investment in our future, allowing for a better educational system, better social programs, a more productive economy, and more employment. There is a direct link, as many studies have shown, between government debt and private-sector output and productivity. Since investment is the usual way through which new technology is introduced into the production process, government debt becomes a vital source of innovation and productivity enhancement. In fact, the productivity slowdown during the 1970s has proved to be the result of the decline in government expenditures.[4]

In this light, attempts to compare the national debt to our personal finances—the idea being, of course, that no individual would, could, or should continue living on such enormous borrowings—must be denounced at once. The comparison, though effective, is misleading. While consumers use credit cards to purchase goods and services, government debt can be used for productive investments. If consumers and entrepreneurs were allowed to borrow funds on their credit cards, for instance, to start a business or to save the family farm, such borrowings would be seen as an investment rather than consumption, and they would create jobs and contribute to the over-all wealth of the economy.

The Myths about Deficits and Debts

Canada's Debt-to-GDP Ratio

We are constantly being reminded by politicians, the media, and the business community that deficits and the debt are out of control and that our debt is now at unprecedented heights. It is argued that our debt-to-GDP ratio of 55 per cent has never been so high, that it is among the highest in the industrialized world, and that if this situation persists, Canada will be no better off than countries such as Argentina and Brazil. The consequences, it is claimed, could be disastrous. International bond-credit agencies do not look favourably upon Canada's economic and financial "mess," and would systematically downgrade Canada's privileged triple-A rating. Canada would then have to pay higher interest rates when borrowing abroad, since it would be considered a bigger risk. If this were to happen, the country would be forced to declare bankruptcy.

While Canadians may be inclined to believe this apocalyptic message, it begs scrutiny of the facts. First, there is the question of whether we can honestly compare the debt-to-GDP ratio between countries. Is it really honest to compare Canada's ratio to, say, that of the United States? What constitutes public spending in one country may not constitute public spending in another. For example, does the United States include unemployment insurance, health care, or transfer payments for post-secondary education in the calculation of its ratio?

Second, although many politicians are preoccupied with Canada's "high" debt-to-GDP ratio, some international bond-credit agencies do not seem to be as concerned. Moody's of New York, an international bond-rating agency, reported in its June, 1993, newsletter, "After an intensive examination of [Canada's] economic and political situation, Moody's confirmed Canada's AAA rating," and it concluded without hesitation that "clearly, the Federal Government's fiscal position is *not* out of control." (Emphasis added.)

Moody's even suggested that the government was misleading Canadians by including certain items in the calculation of the debt that should be excluded. For instance, out of the total debt, we should exclude the part that is owned by the Bank of Canada (almost $30 billion), since it is "the debt of the Federal Government held by the Federal Government"; that is, the Bank of Canada is an arm of the government, so this is money that the government owes itself. The Moody's report also suggests that the government has not been honest with Canadians when it compared Canada's *gross* debt to other countries' *net* debt: "These inaccurate measurements may have played a role in exaggerated evaluations of the severity of Canada's debt problems."

Finally, the most fundamental question of all: Is Canada's debt-to-GDP ratio really at historic heights? The answer is no. Canada experienced levels far higher in the 1930s and after the Second World War, when our debt-to-GDP ratio was almost 110 per cent, which means that we were not producing enough in one year to cover what we owed, largely to ourselves. Mainstream economists point out that this was due to special circumstances, so comparisons between then and now are not reasonable. Perhaps so; however, according to their own logic and ideological arguments, it should not matter how the debt was incurred, only that it was at "alarming" levels. From this perspective, economists, governments, and, in fact, the entire free world should have been up in arms about the financial mess, burdened and crippled as they were under the enormous weight of the debt. It should have put an end to any possible future that Canadians could have hoped for. Was Canada bankrupted? Was there panic? Far from it. In fact, what followed was almost thirty years of nearly uninterrupted economic growth: our standard of living increased significantly, our social safety net expanded, unemployment and inflation were low.

The debt-to-GDP ratio eventually came down to a low of 18.2 per cent, in 1975. It has been rising since, but there is no concrete proof that the cause has been excessive government spending. In fact, as we shall see below, today's situation has very little to do with government spending. It is also obvious that many economists and reputable international bond-credit agencies do not see Canada's situation as a mess, nor as an albatross that threatens our potential to grow, create wealth, or attract international investors.

Taxes and Cutbacks

Another popular myth concerning deficits and debt is that the federal government has only two policy choices at its disposal. It can either raise taxes or reduce spending, since deficits are created solely by a lack of revenue or by overly zealous and wasteful government spending. This has in fact been the government's approach for the past fifteen years.[5]

The federal government has certainly been busy in the tax area. From 1981 to 1991, tax revenues in Canada rose by more than 140 per cent, from a little over $50 billion to more than $122 billion,[6] although not in an equitable way. While personal income tax rose from a low of $19 billion, in 1981, to a high of $70 billion, in 1991, corporate tax rose from $8 billion to only $13 billion over the same period. Over all, as a percentage of GDP, tax revenues rose from 14.3 per cent to 21.7 per cent.

While tax revenues increased, so did expenditures, although at a lower rate. From 1982 to 1991, government expenditures, excluding debt-service charges, rose by 93 per cent, although they remained relatively steady as a percentage of GDP. With growth in revenue greater than growth in expenditures, how can we account for the growth in our deficit and debt? The answer is that there is a third element in the equation.

The deficit and debt have grown in recent years as a result of the high-interest-rate policy of the Bank of Canada. Payment of interest on the debt is a growing problem; if the federal government truly wanted to eliminate deficits and reduce debt, it would be advised to turn to this most obvious source of expenditures.

The federal government recognizes that interest payments have increased considerably over the years, but it claims that this has been caused by excessive debt, not by high interest rates; if the debt were reduced, interest payments would also decrease. Implicit in this argument is that debt pushes up interest rates (to be addressed later). Thus, the only way to reduce interest payments on the debt is to reduce the debt—through tax hikes and expenditure cutbacks. The argument is circular and does not have much empirical evidence to back it up. Interest payments, while obviously linked to the level of debt, are far more dependent on the level of interest rates, as any homeowner will tell you.

Interest-rate relief is a credible third alternative to reducing the debt. When 30 per cent of each tax dollar goes to servicing the debt, it is clearly not an acceptable situation. This is the real cost of government deficits and debt. We need only look at history to understand why. If we compare the growth of the debt and of interest rates over the years, we see that in 1939, while our debt-to-GDP ratio was nearly 110 per cent, our debt was just over $5 billion and interest payments were roughly $150 million, or 3 per cent. By 1992, the debt had grown eighty times, while interest payments increased three hundred times—and our debt-to-GDP ratio was half of what it had been sixty years earlier. Simply put, the numbers do not add up in favour of neoclassical economists' arguments. We are in the middle not of a *fiscal* crisis, but of a *monetary* one, based on our high-interest-rate policy.

Thus, we cannot ignore the impact of the Bank of Canada's restrictive anti-inflationary monetary policy. When we take a closer and disaggregated look at the federal government's finances, we can conclude that the main source of our high deficits is interest payments on the debt. Those who claim that we are in a fiscal crisis are not looking at the whole picture; actually, our fiscal house is very much in order. Mainstream economists prefer to ignore the disaggregated components of fiscal policy, because they realize that if deficits are dissected in such a way, their argument would no longer be valid.

If we exclude interest payments from government expenditures, we end up with what economists call the balance of operations. The advantage of this approach is it gives a clearer and more appropriate picture of the true nature of the government's expenditures related to its consumption and investments. Since 1988, the federal government has been running an operating surplus, a fact proudly defended by our former minister of finance, Don Mazankowski. Granted, our fiscal situation has gotten under control because of major tax increases and expenditure restraints, but the current situation clearly shows that such policies are no longer warranted. In fact, the federal government ran a $12 billion operating surplus in 1991 alone. Since 1988, government surpluses have amounted to more than $40 billion; in 1991, the surplus was $12 billion. It is only when we add the debt charges that we end up with large deficits.

What allowed our debt-to-GDP ratio to come tumbling down after the Second World War was not restraint policies but low interest rates. From 1933 to 1980, our average real interest rate (after taking inflation into account) was only 1.4 per cent. Since 1980, interest rates have soared, thus imposing an enormous burden on the country. Debt charges have more than tripled, and now total more than $300 billion. It is little wonder that after more than ten years of high interest rates, we are unable to reduce our deficit and bring down our soaring debt: "When the federal government has to pay interest on its debt of more than 6% in real terms, as compared with the historic level of 1.4%, its costs are tremendously inflated and controlling the deficit becomes much more difficult."[7] As a 1989 study pointed out, we must examine the growth of the debt and of the debt-to-GDP ratio within its proper historical context, by looking at the factors that influenced that growth. What contributed to the growth of the economy during the postwar years, in addition to reducing the debt-to-GDP ratio, was the fact that the after-tax interest rate was lower than the rate of economic growth, leading to increasing revenues and decreasing costs. This situation was reversed in 1975.[8]

The argument that the government has only two ways of fighting deficits and debt is blatantly false. The federal government could ask the Bank of Canada to reduce the interest rate to its more traditional and historical level. Even the finance department has stated that each reduction of one percentage point in the interest rate would save the government $7 billion. Had this policy been in place since 1980, there is no doubt that deficits would not have existed and that the debt would be much, much lower.

Nonetheless, certain groups and vested interests in society would find reducing the interest rate unacceptable, even dangerous. It would represent a considerable loss in income to those entities, such as banks and large financiers, that are the proprietors of our debt. Indeed, the most important development in our economy over the last fifteen years has been the resurgence of the rentiers and their control over a large part of the economy. Their arguments against lower interest rates must be interpreted in light of the losses that they would incur and their vested interest in defending a tight monetary policy; in short, "powerful vested interests are opposed to very low interest rates."[9]

In light of these arguments, the issue at the centre of debt reduction through lower interest rates is income redistribution. "If governments go into debt simply to pay out interest payments to rich rentiers . . . the consequences would be different than if the debt was incurred in order to transfer money to the poor and the unemployment."[10] In other words, Canada's current debt "problem" benefits the rich and leads increasingly to important constraints being imposed by our "rentier economy."

Keynes was not sympathetic to rentiers, and he likened them to usurers.[11] He blamed them for economic events such as the depression of the 1930s, and believed that their very existence was detrimental to the economy because of their influence over income distribution. Since rentiers have the highest marginal propensity to save, their income contributes to the slowing down of the economy.

What would be an appropriate level for interest rates? This depends on what other programmes or institutional structures are in place to deal with problems that would arise from such a policy. Economists will never agree on a specific level. It is interesting to note, however, that Keynes favoured a 0 per cent real interest rate, primarily because he was against the idea of "rentier capital accumulation."[12]

Those who are against low interest rates argue that the inevitable results would be inflation and a lower Canadian dollar. While the notion of inflation and its causes will be addressed in the next chapter, Canadians might have to accept a lower dollar as a "price" to pay for a lower interest rates, although I am not convinced that interest rates have that strong a link with the value of the Canadian dollar. In fact, there does not seem to be any solid empirical research convincingly demonstrating that the causality is strong.

Inflation

One of the government's main arguments in its fight against the deficit and the debt is that they are inflationary. The logic is the following: more government expenditures lead to increased aggregate demand, which leads, as any introductory economics textbook will show, to higher prices. It is assumed that the general level of prices in the economy is directly determined by the forces of supply and demand. A second argument suggests that as deficits rise, the government would order the printing of more money to pay its bills, which would flood the market and raise prices. Logically, the inverse should also be true: periods of government surpluses should lead to periods of low inflation.

Without dealing here with the true causes of inflation (see chapter four), let us see if, historically, high deficits have been associated with high inflation. If we look at Canada's experience since 1926, economists would be hard-pressed to convince Canadians that there is a causal relationship between deficits, debt, and inflation. Canada's highest inflation rate, 14.3 per cent in 1948, accompanied a period of substantial budgetary surpluses. As well, the growth of the deficit between 1981 and 1985 was accompanied by a decline in the rate of inflation, from 12.4 per cent to 4 per cent.[13] Conversely, during the Second World War, as Canada incurred large deficits, its inflation rate was kept relatively low. And this is not to mention the current situation of low inflation. The bottom line is that there does not seem to be any solid empirical evidence to sustain the assertion that deficits and debt are inflationary.

Discouraging Private Investment

It has been argued by mainstream economists that government spending reduces private investment, in most cases by an equal amount. In what is called the crowding-out effect, in periods of economic growth, as government earmarks money for a specific project, this drives up savings and prevents the private sector from participating in the same project.[14] If firms cannot find other projects in which to invest, and neoclassical theory assumes that they do not, then total investment falls and the economy is harmed, since government investment is inevitably less efficient.

The crowding-out argument goes something like this: deficit spending adds a government demand for savings to an existing private demand—that is, the government will seek buyers for its bonds by competing with the private sector for the fixed available savings. If savings are fixed, the price of savings—the interest rate—must go up, since there is now more demand. Higher interest rates and insufficient savings squeeze out the private sector. If this interpretation is correct, and if, as mainstream economists argue, the private sector is at all times more efficient, government activist fiscal policies should be condemned.

It follows that if government borrowing pushes up interest rates, periods of high deficits should be associated with high interest rates. However, research shows that the "facts of experience" do not support the alleged relationship between deficits, debt, and interest rates.[15] In fact, after peaking in 1981, interest rates have been coming down despite increasing deficits.

The theory does not seem to hold in other countries, either. In the table below, countries are ranked according to two criteria: rate of growth of their national debt and increase in their interest rates. In column one, Canada ranks first, implying that we ran up the biggest cumulative debt, and Great Britain ranks last. The crowding-out argument would lead us to expect the order to be more or less respected in column two—that is, countries with the largest debt accumulation ought to have the greatest growth in interest rates. However, this is not the case. In fact, the results are rather surprising. Canada, with the largest debt accumulation, had the smallest growth in interest rates, while exactly the opposite is true for Great Britain. These results are disconcerting to those who support the idea that larger deficits lead to higher interest rates.

Countries Ranked by Increases in Debt and in Interest Rates
1980–1986[16]

Rank in order of debt increases	Rank in order of increases in interest rates
1. Canada	1. Great Britain
2. France	2. Italy
3. Italy	3. France
4. West Germany	4. United States
5. Japan	5. West Germany
6. United States	6. Japan
7. Great Britain	7. Canada

There thus does not seem to be any solid empirical proof that government deficits crowd out private investment. In fact, as the former chief economist of the U.S. Congressional Budget Office grudgingly admitted, "One would expect a positive relationship between the deficit and real interest rates. This relationship has been devilishly difficult to document statistically."[17]

The crowding-out effect could exist under two very specific theoretical situations. First, if the money supply is fixed—as assumed by neoclassical economists—any increase in the demand for money will likely lead to a rise in the interest rate. Second, if the economy is in a stable, long-run, full-employment equilibrium position, savings would be fixed. By definition, full employment implies a situation in which resources (human and capital) are fully utilized. In such a situation, it may be logical to conclude that government spending discourages private investment, as both sectors would be competing for "limited" resources, including savings. In this "special" case, government spending may not add to national wealth, although it still does not explain how government investments could subtract from overall wealth. However, the problem with this approach is that the economy is seldom, if ever, in a full-employment equilibrium position, no matter how orthodox economists define it. And if the economy were to be in such a situation, it would, as Keynes pointed out, only be temporary. Currently, in the context of a prolonged recession, demand is weak, unemployment is high, and resources are underutilized; it is difficult to see how increased government spending can do more harm than good, or how public investments do not contribute to over-all wealth, especially since private investments are not being undertaken. In fact, contrary to the crowding-out argument, many studies have shown the existence of a "crowding-in" effect: government spending leads to greater private spending.

Foreign Borrowing

It is argued that our debt and deficit are so enormous that we have no choice but to borrow outside of Canada. Luckily, it is agreed, it is this foreign financing of our debt that enables us to continue enjoying our current standard of living; without it, Canada would certainly face horrendous consequences. The arguments with regard to foreign borrowing have been contradictory. For instance, it is feared that if foreign investors are alarmed at the escalation of our debt, they may suddenly decide to stop lending us money. If this were to happen, Canada would be critically short of funds, and the government would be forced to make massive cuts in social programs. In this context, foreign borrowing is seen as beneficial. On the other hand, we have been reminded in recent years that foreign borrowing has increased considerably and we need to reduce our dependence on it. The most frequently proposed solution is not to seek funding within Canada—that possibility is ruled out—but to reduce our deficit at once. Given these two arguments, it is difficult to discern whether foreign borrowing is good or bad.

It is difficult to argue against the dangers of foreign borrowing; in fact, it never should have started in the first place. There are numerous myths regarding this practice. The first one concerns the percentage of the debt owned by foreign powers, and, more importantly, the amounts held in foreign currency. It is true that an increasing share of our debt is owned by foreigners, but almost all of it (96 per cent) is held in Canadian dollars. At the very limit, this is not disastrous, since the value of our debt will fluctuate with the value of our dollar. If the Canadian dollar falls, we will still owe the same amount to foreigners, although they will lose if they exchange Canadian dollars into their own currency. There is reason to worry when the debt is owned in foreign currencies, since the value of that portion of the debt will rise proportionately to the fall of the Canadian currency. At present, however, only 4 per cent of our debt is in foreign currencies (principally Japanese yen, American dollars, and German marks).

The preferred solution is to finance our deficit entirely within Canada. Many economists will argue that this is impossible, since there are not sufficient savings in the hands of Canadians to buy government-issued bonds. This is not true, since there are currently more than $300 billion in bank deposits—almost ten times the average deficit. There is hence no reason to believe the current deficit could not be financed entirely within Canada, as was done to cover much larger wartime deficits.[18]

What if there were not enough savings in Canada to finance the government deficit and debt? To answer this question, we must understand what savings are, and how they are created. In a world of money, as opposed to a world in which commodities are exchanged for commodities, savings are what is left after consumption; aggregate savings are the total savings in the economy. There can be no savings unless there is income; unemployed workers cannot save. Thus, savings can be generated through the creation of employment and income. When the unemployment rate is as high as it is now, aggregate saving is lower than if we were closer to full employment.

Why, then, has there been foreign borrowing? The federal government finances its deficit by issuing various bonds, which can be purchased by foreigners (except for Canada Savings Bonds). With high interest rates, bonds become very attractive to foreigners, as the potential gains are high. There is, however, a second and more interesting reason, which affects principally provincial governments. Since borrowing entails interest payments, it is quite logical for provincial governments to seek financing where the interest rate is most favourable. The structure of Canadian interest rates since the early 1980s has been designed precisely to force provinces to seek cheaper financial arrangements outside Canada, where interest rates are generally lower.

The Burden Left to Future Generations
Many Canadians have come to believe that the public debt will eventually cripple the well-being and standard of living of our children and grandchildren, since they will have to pay for our "extravagant" spending through higher taxes. We are constantly

reminded that every Canadian is born owing many thousand of dollars.

This argument could have merit, if governments and the Bank of Canada continue to adopt economic policies based on neoclassical hypotheses, as they have in the last two decades. Of course, if interest rates are kept artificially high, the debt will plague generations to come. However, there is reason to believe that debt is not a burden to future generations. In fact, the biggest burden we can leave our grandchildren is to leave them no debt at all. Provided that debt is incurred primarily through public investment rather than consumption, there is no reason to believe that it is a burden. We need to determine the type of society that we want to leave future generations, and then undertake the proper investments. "Indeed, there is only one way in which we can allow today to injure tomorrow. That is to act today so that tomorrow has less productive capital."[19]

When governments invest in better and stronger infrastructure, education systems, human-resources training, research and development, and other social programs, they are actually investing in our future, not taking away from it. Thus, "To the extent that part of what the government spends goes for physical investments [infrastructure spending] . . . financing such expenditures by borrowing is no more than what any business putting up a new plant typically does—or any family building a new house."[20] What kind of future would we leave our children if we did not undertake investments in these fields? "Those future generations . . . will be much worse off if, instead of a deficit, we leave them a country plagued by ill-health, poverty, joblessness, decrepit schools, and a crumbling infrastructure. A balanced budget will not be viewed as an adequate substitute for social and economic security."[21] Through productive debt, we leave future generations a better and stronger society and an increased capital stock.

Those who believe that government debt is a burden to future generations are comparing the government to a private-sector firm. For a business, debt is owed to outsiders; when a firm reimburses its debt to the bank, it settles a financial obligation to an outside claimant on its property. In the case of the government, the situation is radically different. The debt is largely owed to ourselves; when the government pays out interest or pays back the debt, it essentially gives back into the community from which it levied the tax in the first place—although it also favours the rentiers. If the government decided to reimburse all of its debt (if it could), the national economy and the community would still not be rid of its obligation to an outside claimant. Society as a whole would not be any wealthier or better off; some individuals would be better off, but at the expense of others. Since the money is owed to ourselves, there would be no elimination of the burden to future generations, since no burden existed initially. If we ever repaid the debt, the generation that paid it off would be the one that received the proceeds. Those who claim otherwise either are ignorant of the nature of debt or simply interested in personal gains.

Policy Implications

To say that debt is of no consequence is a foolish statement; however, there is no reason to fear it when it is used in productive ways. We should not see the debt as a monolithic rock around our necks. If used properly, it can propel Canada on a prosperous path into the twenty-first century. What needs to be understood is how the current debt is preventing us from investing in our future. Since 1982, Canadians have paid almost $350 billion in interest payments alone. This speaks volumes about the waste that our current policies are producing. The rise of the public debt over the past two decades has not been caused by extensive government spending, but by excessively high real interest rates. Governments must therefore adopt a strategy that reduces the waste associated with the current anti-inflation policy. The only credible solution is to lower interest rates. This policy would not please certain vested interests, such as the rentiers, but it would go a long way toward ameliorating Canada's situation. Canadians may have to accept a lower dollar, but they should be informed of the benefits that this would bring. Many economists already acknowledge that our dollar is overvalued. For instance, Quebec economist Pierre Fortin, in an interview in *L'Actualité* (1 March 1993), noted that our dollar should be allowed to fall to "70 cents, or even 60 cents."

Some are quick to point out that a lower dollar would be inflationary. If mainstream economists were honest with themselves, they would realize, however, that their own model does not support their view. For them, inflation is caused by excess money, not by a low value for the Canadian dollar (see next chapter). Simply put, inflation is not caused by low interest rates.

There is much to be done and discussed, of course, when it comes to the question of the debt. The most crucial thing, I believe, is to understand where it comes from and how it is created. To do this, it is important to realize that government spending is not all consumption and that the state has an important, if not vital, role to play in investing in our future.

Many economists believe that we should rethink the way deficits are counted by separating consumption and investment, and there is certainly good reason to believe that this is a valid and logical way of accounting for government fiscal policy. (After all, the private sector already calculates its profits in such a way. There is no doubt that if firms calculated their profits in the same way governments calculate their deficits, they would be in a perpetual deficit situation.) Expenditures within the capital account are investments undertaken in areas, such as education, infrastructure, and research and development, in which society benefits from the positive externalities associated with public investment. Such expenditures also contribute to an over-all increase in the standard of living of all Canadians through employment creation and increased productivity.

In the *Treasury Memoranda*, which contains his postwar employment-policy ideas, Keynes clearly favoured government economic policies that encourage investment rather than consumption, and the government's role in encouraging capital accumulation. But, as with many other ideas which Keynes put forward, the subtle difference between consumption and investment was lost in the later "Keynesian" policies. One need only glance through any introductory textbook to see that, in fact, traditional "Keynesian" aggregate-demand analysis considers all government spending to be a single component. Keynes did not see fiscal policy as a series of short-term counter-cyclical "quick-fix" measures of the type that governments have a tendency to adopt. Rather, investments should be long term, in order to address the economy's real structural problems. In this context, Keynes would not have approved of government subsidies and fiscal exemptions, viewing them largely as inefficient and wasteful and as leading to speculative investment, mergers, and acquisitions. The notion that any type of government intervention is of a "Keynesian" nature is false, and can be attributed to the "bastard" Keynesian policies that were made popular by economists who did not understand Keynes's ideas.

Keynes believed that because of uncertainty and the existence of money, capitalist economies cannot produce the necessary level of investment to guarantee sustainable economic growth and full employment. This is why, in the *General Theory*, he emphasized the need for the "socialization of investment."[22]

We should not associate Keynes's terms with the Marxian principle of state-owned means of production. Keynes's view "should not be construed as trying to attain, in the final analysis, the state ownership of all the means of production in conformity with Marxian principles. Keynes's proposal in favour of public investment has to do with the *composition* of government expenditures."[23] Keynes argued not that the government should own factories, businesses, or plants, but that it should stimulate or "organize" investment, funneling resources to the most prosperous areas of the economy. He posited that there is a fundamental conflict between entrepreneurs and rentiers, whose destabilizing role stems from their lack of any long-term vision, which makes investment financing difficult. By blocking access to initial financing, rentiers often control the destinies of entrepreneurs and prevent them from investing and thus contributing to economic growth. The state therefore has a legitimate role to play in "organizing" investment and putting an end to rentiers' control over credit and finance.

To guarantee the "euthanasia of rentiers,"[24] whose interests often go against the interests of society as a whole, Keynes suggested that governments influence "two-thirds to three-fourths"[25] of total investment in the economy. This policy is certainly one of his most controversial and radical ideas. Whether the proposed proportion is appropriate is open to discussion. What is important is to understand the need for government involvement in the economy—as a "guiding influence"—and the positive results of proper public investment. This is why it is important to differentiate between consumption and investments, the latter being, according to Keynes, self-financing in the long run.[26]

Thus, while debt reduction may well be an important economic objective for the years to come, it should not be pursued for the reasons advocated by certain vested interests. The money that would be saved through lower interest rates should be put toward a great number of public investment projects, which, I am sure, would not be difficult to identify. Blindly pursuing debt reduction would create a far greater economic mess: "It will benefit Canadians not at all if the price we pay for getting the financial deficit under control is the decline of our health care, our education, our social programmes, and our public sector. These are the 'deficits' we really should be concerned about."[27]

The experience of the last fifteen years stands as a testimony to the brutal economic policies of the federal government. Every attempt to reduce the deficit has only made things worse. The conclusions must be clear to all: deficit reduction is achieved by initially increasing the deficit in order to create employment, thereby increasing revenues. Is it legitimate to ask whether more taxes and cutbacks are the only possible alternatives for governments that want to reduce their debt? Is it wrong to believe that government cutbacks may in fact worsen the situation, especially when they are undertaken during a recession? As Canada's current minister of state for international financial institutions, Doug Peters, recently stated, "By cutting expenditures, by adjusting programmes, you will not get out of the deficit. You will end up with as big or large deficits each time you try."[28] In recent years, in attempting to control the growing debt by cutting expenditures, governments have exacerbated the problem. The real problem is not government expenditures, but interest payments.

It is perhaps fitting to close this chapter with the wise words of American Nobel Prize laureate economist James Tobin:

> Deficit reduction is not an end in itself. Its rationale is to improve productivity, real wages, and living standards of our children and their children. If the measures to cut deficits actually diminish GDP, raise unemployment, and reduce future-oriented activities of government, business and households, they do not achieve the goals that are their raison-d'être; rather they retard them. This perverse result is likely if deficit reduction measures are introduced while the economy is as weak and as constrained by effective demand as it is now.[29]

Notes

1. For a thorough yet very accessible discussion of the debt, see Heilbroner and Bernstein, *The Debt and the Deficit*.
2. Chorney, Hotson, and Seccareccia, *The Deficit Made Me Do It*.
3. *Globe and Mail*, editorial, 17 Feb. 1993.
4. For instance, see Munnel, "Is there too little," pp. 4–5.
5. See Lavoie, "L'idéologie des discours budgétaires fédéraux."
6. *Public Accounts*, various years. Quoted in Abele, *How Ottawa Spends 1992–1993*, p. 394.
7. Chorney, Hotson, and Seccareccia, *The Deficit Made Me Do It*, p. 8.
8. Coulombe, *La dynamique de la dette publique*.
9. J. Robinson, *Introduction to the Theory of Employment*, p. 63.
10. Seccareccia and Sharpe, "Déficits budgétaires et compétitivité du Canada."
11. Keynes, *Collected Writings*, vol. 21, p. 412.

12. This expression was used by Seccareccia and Lavoie in "Les idées révolution-naires de Keynes," p. 59.

13. Bellan, "Les déficits budgétaires fédéraux."

14. See, for example, Spencer and Yoke, "The 'Crowding-out Effect.'"

15. See Wray, "L'effet d'éviction," and Bellan, "Les déficits budgétaires."

16. Bernstein, Peter (1988) "All the Things Deficits Don't Do."

17. Penner, "The Economics," p. 8.

18. I am relying on figures quoted by Ruben Bellan in an *Ottawa Citizen* article on 26 Apr. 1993, p. A13.

19. Eisner, "Budget Deficits," p. 76.

20. B. Friedman, *Day of Reckoning*, p. 88.

21. Chorney, Hotson, and Seccareccia, *The Deficit Made Me Do It*, p. 14.

22. See chapter 24 in the *General Theory* (Keynes, *Collected Writings*, vol. 7). Also see the *Treasury Memoranda* (ibid., vol. 8) and The *End of Laissez-Faire* (ibid., vol. 9).

23. Seccareccia, *Keynesianism and Public Investment,* p. 10.

24. Keynes, *Collected Writings*, vol. 7, p. 22.

25. Ibid., vol. 27, p. 322.

26. Ibid., vol. 27, pp. 320–2.

27. Chorney, Hotson, and Seccareccia, *The Deficit Made Me Do It*, p. 3.

28. Doug Peters, comments made to the House of Commons Standing Committee on Finance. Minutes of Proceedings and Evidence of the Standing Committee on Finance, 31 May 1993, p. 10.

29. Quoted by Doug Peters in Minutes of Proceedings and Evidence of the Standing Committee on Finance during testimony, 31 May 1993, p. 5.

CHAPTER FOUR

INFLATION:
FROM AUSTERITY TO INSTITUTIONALISM

Over the last two decades, inflation has become one of the most dominant policy issues on the Canadian public agenda, and successive fiscal and monetary policies have been largely aimed at either controlling or reducing it. Governments and the Bank of Canada have somehow been under the impression that increases in the general price level are directly related to the policies they have adopted.

We all know what inflation is. Simply put, it is a general increase in the aggregate level of prices, as measured by a number of indicators, the most frequently quoted of which is the Consumer Price Index. However, economists cannot agree on what causes inflation. As with other issues in this book, there are two basic schools of thought, each with its own set of principles, causes, and solutions. The differences are enormous, and most probably irreconcilable. On the one hand are the monetarists,[1] whose philosophy is based on neoclassical principles, and who are convinced that inflation is caused by the quantity of money circulating in the economy. On the other hand are the post-Keynesians, who view inflation as a social and institutional problem of income distribution.

The policies ultimately adopted to fight inflation are based on one particular view and understanding of inflation and how it occurs, and of the threats it represents to certain groups within society. The adoption of one specific policy rather than another might bring benefits to some, while imposing hardship on others. In most cases, those who wield more power within society will be in a better position to influence the direction of both fiscal and monetary policies.

In general, the fight against inflation has been left largely in the hands of the Bank of Canada. In recent years, there has been tremendous consensus among economists that the Bank's current policies of austerity are wrong. By attempting to cure one ill, it has created many more important ones. With its policy of high interest rates, the Bank of Canada can be held responsible for the "planned" recessions of the 1980s and 1990s. On top of contributing to high interest-service charges on the debt, the Bank's anti-inflationary restrictive monetary policy has also led to high unemployment, decreased productive investments, increased speculative investments, a higher Canadian dollar, low economic growth, and reduced consumer confidence in the economy. Even the editor-in-chief of the *Globe and Mail*, William Thorsell, admitted that the Bank of Canada's tight money policy has done "substantial and unnecessary harm to the economy" (*Globe and Mail*, 10 July 1993).

The Bank of Canada was not always obsessed with inflation. In fact, its mandate clearly states that its objectives ought to be price stability, economic growth, and low unemployment. At one time, central bankers in Canada were concerned with all three objectives, and carefully balanced one against the other. However, the inflation of the 1970s, despite being coupled with high unemployment, quickly turned that around; in 1973, the Bank of Canada officially declared itself monetarist.

As stated above, by attempting solely to fight inflation, the Bank of Canada actually created more important problems. This is certainly not a "true" Keynesian approach to macro-economic policy, since Keynes's philosophy was not to solve one problem in order to create another one. In fact, "Keynes's entire intellectual commitment was to use reason to eradicate economic ailments rather than to 'trade-off' one ill for another."[2] Economic policy, whether fiscal or monetary, should be aimed at solving several problems simultaneously. Unfortunately, this is not what Canadians have been witnessing in recent years.

Monetarism, Inflation, and the Politics of Austerity

Orthodox economists see the world as a monolithic market of perfectly competitive, profit-maximizing firms, and regard the actions of significant real-world institutions, such as organized commodity and financial markets, commercial banks, and organized labour, as theoretically insignificant or negligible. These abstractions make it easier to see inflation as being "always and everywhere a monetary phenomenon," to use Milton Friedman's expression. This means that increases in the general price level are caused by an excessive amount of money in the economy—that is, "too much money chasing too few goods." Economists often use the following example to illustrate this theory: Assume the existence of only apples and money in the economy. There are 200 apples, and $200 floating around. Each apple would then cost $1. Now assume that the stock of money doubles to $400 (the Bank of Canada decides to print more money); each apple would now be worth $2, hence inflation, due to an "overissue" of bank notes, to use Ricardo's expression. Of course, this analogy assumes that the production of apples remains constant. Nonetheless, the model accurately reflects the neoclassical/monetarist hypothesis that money is the cause of inflation. Believing that this was the primary—indeed, the only—cause of inflation, Friedman argued that by controlling the growth in money supply, central banks could effectively control growth in the general level of prices.[3] So powerful was this idea, and so apparently simple as well, that it swept across North America and most industrialized countries. Other heterodox economists argue that monetarism conquered the world not because of its simplicity, but because it allowed certain vested interests to gain back the power they lost during the postwar years of low unemployment. This is my argument as well.

The idea that inflation is a monetary phenomenon rests upon a number of hypotheses, most of which are dubious at best. A review of these hypotheses demonstrates the incompatibility between theory and practice.

93

Money as a "Veil"

In a neoclassical world, money, which is considered to be like any other commodity, does not play a significant role in determining the real dimensions of the economy. It does not enter into any models dealing with production and is not allowed to influence the behaviour of economic agents. In such a world, based on Say's Law (see chapter two), goods are exchanged for goods, and money is only used to facilitate this process; this is what economists call a pure exchange economy. Money was introduced to reduce transaction costs; it is simply a "veil," to use Mill's expression, behind which the real economy operates unhampered by considerations of a financial nature. Since this is the case, according to monetarists, any decrease in the money stock can only result in a decrease in the general price level and cannot affect the real dimensions of the economy, such as level of income, investment, production, or employment. As Friedman stated, "We accepted the quantity theory presumptions, and have thought it was supported by the evidence examined, that changes in the quantity of money as such *in the long run* have a negligible effect on real income, so that non-monetary forces are 'all that matter' for real income over decades and 'money does not matter.'"[4] The "money as a veil" assumption has since been more accurately referred to as the "neutrality of money," and it remains at the heart of orthodox thinking.

This is precisely the philosophy that governs the Bank of Canada's current monetary policy. In its defence, monetarists argue that any adverse effects this restrictive monetary policy might have on the economy are only temporary, and in the long run the economy will find its way back to equilibrium due to the "invisible hand" of the market. In the end (when we are all dead, as Keynes pointed out), the economy will be healthier and consumers will be better off.

Keynes rejected the validity of the "neutrality of money" dictum, and he argued that money plays a far greater role in our economy than monetarists would like to admit. It can be held for speculative reasons, or for no reason at all. It is the decision to hold money against the uncertainty of the future that has puzzled economists. Simply put, "Money matters." As an important component of a monetary economy of production, it is used as a means of settling contractual obligations. Keynes wrote, in 1933,

> An economy which uses money but uses it merely as a neutral link between transactions in real things and real assets and does allow it to enter into motives and decision, might be called—for want of a better name—a real-exchange economy. The theory which I desiderate would deal, in contradistinction to this, with an economy in which money plays a part of its own and affects motives and decisions and is, in short, one of the operative factors in the situation, so that the course of events cannot be predicted either in the long period or in the short, without knowledge of the behaviour of money between the first state and the last. And it is this which we ought to mean when we speak of a monetary economy.[5]

Because production takes time and contracts are honoured in the future, money is a necessary factor for firms; it is needed to pay workers and to meet contractual obligations when they come due during production. (The post-Keynesian emphasis on production is explained in chapter two.) Contrary to orthodox thinking, money is not neutral and can be the cause of much instability. In a world of uncertainty, money is held as an asset as well as a store of wealth. Since most contracts, including wages, are denominated in terms of money, an immediate command over money can be a sensible way of dealing with situations in which the future money value of real and financial assets may decline. Faced with this uncertainty, firms may decide to hold money rather than invest it. In this regard, Keynes saw money as a link between an irreversible past and an unknown future: producers use it to protect themselves against the possible erroneous spending decisions of consumers. As well, since expectations of sales and profits can fall short of realized results (in both the short and long terms), firms desire liquidity (money) to avoid the effects of possible unpleasant and unexpected events in the future.

Some fifty years later, Keynes's argument was reprised:

> Money has always been an awkward puzzle for neoclassical . . . theory. . . . The holding of intrinsically useless paper as a store of value is a puzzle . . . [yet] common sense tells us money is held and has value. . . . It is not easy to incorporate this common-sense observation in the standard paradigm. . . . The makeshift compromise in neoclassical theory has been the alleged neutrality of money. . . . The application of this neutrality proposition to actual real-world monetary policies is a prime example of the fallacy of misplaced concreteness.[6]

Without doubt, money plays a causal role in economic output. What must be examined is the nature of money and how it can be used in shaping entrepreneurs' motives and behaviour.

Control of the Money Stock

Implicit to Friedman's theory is the notion that the central bank can effectively and directly control the stock of money in the economy, thus controlling inflation, because the causality is direct. The supply of money is hence considered exogenous to the economy. Friedman used the analogy of a helicopter descending from the sky full of money, "manna from Heaven."[7] No matter what happens in the economy—whether the demand for money increases, investments decrease, unemployment goes up, or deficits get "out of control"—the money supply is unaffected. The central bank can single-handedly decide to increase or decrease the availability of money in the economy. What is seen as beyond the Bank's control is the interest rate, which, in neoclassical theory, is a consequence of the chosen growth rate of the money supply. The forces of supply and demand operate to determine simultaneously both the quantity and the price—the interest rate—of money, much as they do for any other commodity.

It is therefore not difficult to see that any decrease in the supply of money makes it scarcer, hence pushing up its price. Similarly, an increase in the demand is a result of it being more desirable, and also pushes up its price. Because money does not "grow on trees" and its availability is limited (recall the importance of scarcity in neoclassical theory), its price must be allowed to rise to guarantee equilibrium, or else central bankers would face a shortage of funds. At a higher price, some investors will be discouraged and will not demand it any more. The interest rate is thus seen as a price that creates equilibrium between the supply of and demand for money. While a rise in the interest rate is seen as a result of a tight monetary policy, it is thought to be the price to pay for lower inflation.

The idea that the Bank of Canada can directly control the stock of money or its growth rate is not universally accepted. Many economists, among them post-Keynesians, argue that the central bank has no control over the money stock, but does have control over the interest rate. This view, which goes back to the doctrine widely defended in the nineteenth century, is referred to today as the theory of endogenous money.

Where does money come in? Why does it exist? In a production economy such as ours, is it really logical to believe that money comes in only when goods are being exchanged or that it comes from heaven? Or is it more realistic to believe that it comes in during the production process? The question is an important one. If we conclude that money—or, rather, credit-money—is an essential component of production, then the conclusions we reach concerning the alleged control of the money supply could shed some light on the appropriate policies to adopt—or, rather, *not* to adopt—in order to fight inflation.

From this perspective, the economy must be seen as a "circuit" in which credit-money plays a most important role. Firms cannot produce, expand production, buy raw materials, or hire and pay labour without access to some sort of credit. Credit-money is needed before production even starts. When firms demand money, commercial banks supply them with credit. Indeed, in the real world, "bank credit is the primary model of financing productive activity."[8] The logic is as follows. Since production takes time, firms will not reap the rewards of their productive activities until some time in the future, when goods are sold and revenues received. However, in order for those goods to be produced, firms must hire workers and remunerate them. It is thus imperative that they have access to a "wage fund." Any production or capital accumulation requires initial financing. Unlike in neoclassical theory, investments are not financed through savings, but through the banking system; there is no need for prior saving. This independence of investment from saving is at the heart of Keynes's radical departure from orthodoxy.

The private sector's access to financing and credit enables firms to make productive investments and remunerate their workers. Commercial banks are therefore central to the level of investment in the economy. The initial funding they provide allows firms to expand production, honour their contracts, and pay their workers. The income generated is then redeposited in individual accounts in commercial banks. Thus, income occurs because there is an initial investment; bank deposits grow because borrowings have grown. The chain of causality runs from loans to deposits, rather than the other way. Since the money stock in the economy is defined as bank deposits and the sum of money held by economic agents, the money stock is increased. At this point, the economic "circuit" allows money to be created. There is no direct control over the supply of money by the central bank; money is created through access to credit, which is then dispersed as income; in other words, the increased money stock is a result of investment decisions by firms. "This flow of money is endogenous; it is the result of the credit needs of firms, consequent to their production plans."[9] The stock of money is therefore determined by demand, not supply. This challenges the validity of the Bank of Canada's attempts to fight inflation through a restrictive monetary policy.

The fact that the Bank of Canada has no direct control over the growth of money in the economy does not mean that it is powerless. It can impose stringent credit controls by raising interest rates beyond the means of entrepreneurs. However, this does not alter the fact that, even severely constrained, money is created through credit, not through the whims of the Bank of Canada. For central banks, "Their control instrument is a price, not a quantity."[10] The interest rate therefore is exogenous, and is not determined by the forces of supply of and demand for money, but by the central bank's will to let the money supply grow. (Keynes admitted as much when he stated that the "monetary authorities can have any rate of interest they like."[11]) It must then be prepared to "accommodate" any increase in the demand for credit. At a given interest rate, commercial banks will increase their loans until their excess reserves are reduced to none. If firms need more credit, banks will attempt to increase their deposits or will borrow from the central bank. As the "lender of last resort," the central bank must lend the needed funds to the banks at a given interest rate, "over which [commercial] banks set a mark-up when they fix the lending rates."[12] The central bank's role as "lender of last resort" is crucial to capitalism; if it ever refused to honour its obligations, the economy would face a severe financial crisis. Thus, the central bank

> cannot *refuse* the discounting of "eligible bills" rendered to it. If it did, by setting a fixed limit to the amount of bills which the Bank is prepared to discount on a daily or a weekly basis . . . the Bank would fail in its function as "lender of last resort" to the banking system which is essential to ensure that the clearing banks do not become insolvent as a result of a lack of liquidity. Precisely because the monetary authorities cannot afford the disastrous consequences of a collapse of the banking system . . . the "money supply" in a credit-money economy is *endogenous*, not exogenous—it varies in direct response to changes in the public "demand" to hold cash, and bank deposits and independently of that demand.[13]

This approach has led one economist to claim that the interest rate is a politically determined distributional variable rather than a price determined by the market.[14] In this sense, there can never be an "excess" supply of money, since the money supply is always equal to demand.

The power of central banks is nonetheless enormous, and their monetary policies do have a tremendous impact on the economy, even in the long run, despite neoclassical claims to the contrary. High interest rates eventually slow down the economy, as they have done presently. In *The Economic Consequences of Mr. Churchill*, Keynes argued that monetary policies of austerity were policies from which "any humane or judicious person must shrink" and were "simply a campaign against the standard of life of the working classes," operating through the "deliberate intensification of unemployment . . . by using the weapon of economic necessity against individuals and against particular industries—a policy which the country would never permit if it knew what was being done."[15] This is why monetarism has been called a "scourge throughout the world."[16]

Increases in the money supply should be interpreted not as inflationary, but as a positive sign of a healthy economy. As the money stock increases with production, there is no reason to believe that this would necessarily cause inflation. What it does show is the weakness of the monetarists' "apple" analogy, in which inflation occurs only because the production of apples remains stable. This is not a realistic assumption. Production is always going on, so that while the stock of money has increased to $400, the production of apples may have increased to four hundred. In this case, each apple would still be worth a dollar: the money stock rises because production rises. Given this perspective, the reduction in growth of the money supply in recent years must not be interpreted as a victory over inflation, but as a sure sign of the slowing of our economy as the private sector postpones, or simply abandons, any desire to expand production, increase capital, or hire additional labour.

The credit-driven growth in the money supply can also be attributed to increased wages, a theory pioneered by American economist Sidney Weintraub, who suggested that the money stock may increase because firms must find additional funds to finance ongoing production under wage-increase demands. As wage increases translate into higher costs and, therefore, prices, the increase in money supply (as a result of credit needs) will be linked to inflation. However, the difference between this approach and that of monetarists lies in the causality. While monetarists claim that the causality runs from money supply to prices, the facts of the real world suggest the contrary—that the causality runs first from wages, to prices and credit needs, to the money supply: "Changes in wages and unemployment largely determine the demand for bank loans, which in turn determine the rate of growth of the money stock."[17]

Inflation: An Institutionalist Approach

It is clear that the causes of inflation are not those espoused by monetarists and neoclassical economists. (As a result, the Bank of Canada's policy should be viewed with much skepticism.) "The most obvious impact of an endogenous credit money theory is on the theory of inflation. Since the supply of money is *not* an exogenous variable, it cannot be held responsible for the general increase in prices. Inflation cannot be caused by an excessive rate of growth of the supply of money due to incompetent central bankers or to a favourable trade balance. Some other theory of inflation, different from the standard monetarist and now neoclassical view, must be provided."[18]

If inflation is not caused by an excess stock of money, what does cause it? First, we must consider inflation for what it is: an increase in the prices of commodities produced by firms. More basic and fundamental questions then emerge, such as what governs increases in commodity prices, and how production costs enter into the equation. Economists should therefore concern themselves less with a theory of inflation, *per se,* and turn their attention toward a theory of prices and how they are determined.

It is clear that prices are not determined by the stock of money in the economy, and rises in prices are not determined by the growth of the money stock. Furthermore, we must reject the prevailing idea that prices are somehow determined by the market forces of supply and demand,[19] because this rests on certain dubious assumptions about the behaviour of individual economic agents—households and firms. The problems of the supply-and-demand analysis essentially involve identification and time. Economists are aware that it is difficult to measure these curves empirically. What do they look like? What is their shape? What are their slopes? These are all questions beyond the reach of even the most sophisticated modeling techniques. As for calendar time, we know that production takes time, and the idea that demand and supply can interact simultaneously is difficult to accept.

There is another reason that neoclassical supply-and-demand analysis is unable to explain inflation. The very notion of scarcity, upon which neoclassical theory is based, cannot be an acceptable or realistic cause for inflation since, in most markets, firms' rate of capacity utilization is usually less than 100 per cent (full capacity), implying that firms do not respond to "excess" demand by pushing up prices, but rather by increasing production. "Excess demand provides at most a minor component of a comprehensive explanation" for inflation.[20] Even Alfred Marshall, the father of supply-and-demand analysis, grew increasingly uncomfortable with the use of such tools as an end in itself, and warned of its dangers: "When pushed to its more remote and intricate logical consequences, it slips away from the conditions of real life. Its limitations are so constantly overlooked, especially by those who approach it from an abstract point of view, that there is a danger in throwing it into definite form at all."[21]

Before turning to the question of inflation as perceived by post-Keynesians and other heterodox economists, a few issues must be addressed.

The Nature of Markets

In the real world, markets are not dominated exclusively by small, competitive firms whose prices and production quantities are determined solely by the law of supply and demand. Competition is important, since it exists; to reject the idea would in itself be unrealistic. But for Post-Keynesians, competition must be regarded as a process in which resources are allocated and income is distributed between social classes over time.

In the real world, markets can be divided into two broad categories: a relatively small, "perfectly competitive" segment and an oligopolistic segment. The first is limited to "raw materials and foodstuffs,"[22] and in it prices are determined in much the same way as spelled out in orthodox theory. In the over-all scheme of things, its influence on price levels is negligible. The oligopolistic segment is the dominant feature of modern capitalist economies. It is characterized by large firms, which hold a certain "monopoly power" over "administered" prices, and by finished goods, or "commodities produced by means of other commodities." To understand variations in prices—and hence inflation—economists must turn their attention to the formation of prices in the oligopolistic, or primary, sector, not in the competitive sector.

In the primary sector, prices tend to be more rigid. Instead of lowering prices during recessions, oligopolistic firms are believed to have the power to resist such pressures. We should recall that in neoclassical theory an oversupply of or a shortage of demand for a good necessarily lowers its price so that it can be sold. Similarly, if demand is too great, prices tend to be pushed upward to eliminate any possible shortages. Market clearing is guaranteed by price flexibility, and this is the only role of prices. In the real world, however, prices are not an equilibrium mechanism, and do not adjust to any supply or demand excesses. Since prices are fixed, adjustments are made through changes in volume of output. "The administered price thesis significantly held that in business recessions administered prices showed a tendency not to fall as much as market prices, while the recession fall in demand worked itself out primarily through a fall in sales, production and employment. Similarly . . . administered prices . . . tended not to rise as much in recovery while rising demand worked itself out primarily in a rising volume of sales, production and employment."[23] As John Hicks put it, "We suspend the rule that prices must change whenever there is an excess of supply and demand."[24] However, administered prices are not *necessarily* related to the increased number of oligopolies in the market *per se*, but rather to the "greater power of firms over consumers."[25] For example, the growing complexity of products, the technological innovations in them, and their multiplicity are such that consumers are unable to accurately assess the "quality-to-cost ratio" of a given good. Despite this slight variation, the conclusion is the same: the existence of oligopolistic firms with power over the price of their commodity is ignored in neoclassical theory. Since they constitute the dominant feature of a modern capitalist market, any realistic economic theory must deal with the way modern firms operate and, especially, their pricing behaviour. These firms are at the heart of post-Keynesian market theory.

Inflation and Income Distribution
Income distribution is one of the core elements of post-Keynesian economic theory; as it is an integral feature of economic activity, it can often be manipulated by those who wield more influence and power in society. Inflation is also seen in this perspective, as it is considered to be primarily a question of the distribution of income, both as a cause and as a consequence.[26] This view has it that inflation "arises from conflicting views about the proper distribution of income."[27] Income is divided essentially between three groups—workers, owners of capital, and rentiers—who are engaged in a constant struggle to preserve their respective share of total income. As over-all income in society grows, each group will attempt to obtain a larger share of the increase. To understand better the distributional aspect of inflation, let us consider the

mechanics involved by assuming, for the time being, the existence of only two groups: workers and firms.

What are prices? The price a firm charges consumers for its good represents a revenue for that firm. Every price is ultimately somebody's income. When prices rise, there is inflation, and the revenue of firms also rises, so that their share of total income in the economy increases. At the same time, however, increased prices are directly related to workers' real income, or purchasing power; because their income is fixed, they can purchase less. There thus exists, with a given level of aggregate income, an inverse relationship between profits of firms and the wage income of workers.

In a world of competing forces, this creates a definite problem, as each group is bent on preserving its relative share of available national (and international) income. Groups that wield greater influence or power will be able to use it to their advantage. Inflation is therefore not only a question of distribution, but a question of redistribution "*from* weaker groups to the more powerful."[28] As this lopsided distribution takes place, other groups demand increases in their income. Unfortunately, weaker groups do not have the power or influence to increase their income and well-being, so they are often disadvantaged.

How are prices determined? There are two components to prices—cost and mark-up. Before charging consumers a certain price, a firm will take into consideration its total production costs, both fixed and variable, such as wages and the costs of raw materials (costs that fluctuate with production). An "acceptable" profit margin is then added on to generate the needed profits from expected sales to finance initial investment expenditures. This is called internal funding. Unlike neoclassical economic theory, in which investments are financed exclusively through consumers' savings, in the real world, investments are financed through a two-stage process: access to credit (initial funding) and sales revenue (final funding). Further, in post-Keynesian theory, the initial investment itself will generate the needed revenue to finance it.

This makes it clear that the real goal of a firm is not profit maximization, but growth or revenue maximization.[29]

The mark-up approach offers certain definite advantages to firms. By applying a fixed-percentage mark-up over costs, they are guaranteed that the relationship between wholesale and retail prices remains constant in the short term, whenever there are fluctuations in either demand or supply.

How do prices rise? Since wages comprise the largest production cost, their influence on prices is the greatest. Any increase in wages is likely to lead to an increase in prices. Wages increase primarily in two ways. First, if workers believe that they are losing ground in the distributional struggle, they try to increase their standard of living by demanding higher wages, thus adding considerably to the firm's production costs. The firm is then faced with two options: either absorb the higher costs and the new distribution of income, or pass the increased costs onto consumers through higher prices. In most cases, since firms have control over their prices, and since they will not accept any distribution of income that hinders them, they raise their price. As costs are passed on and prices rise, workers face a decline in their real wage, possibly to the extent of canceling out previous gains. Of course, if the rise in prices is greater than that in wages, workers will be worse off than before the initial nominal wage increase. Once the cycle is started and workers resist real wage declines, the economy can be caught in a wage-price spiral. "In the real world of oligopolistic firms and of collective bargaining, firms and workers have some power to change prices and wages. Dissatisfaction with the existing wages and prices may then lead to increases in those wages and prices."[30]

A second source of wage increases is workers' relative wages, not in regard to firms, but between themselves. Keynes noted that groups of workers are most preoccupied with wages earned by other groups. If one group is perceived to be increasing its income relative to other groups, it will not take long for the other groups to demand matching wage increases in order to re-establish the "equilibrium." This is called the wage-wage spiral. As Keynes noted in the *General Theory*, "Any individuals or groups of individuals, who consent to a reduction of money-wages relatively to others, will suffer a *relative* reduction in real wages, which is a sufficient justification for them to resist it. In other words, the struggle about money-wages primarily affects the *distribution* of the aggregate real wage between different labour-groups. . . . The effect of combination on the part of a group of workers is to protect their *relative* real wage."[31]

The inflation of the 1970s was a good example of how these forces can interact. When, in 1973, OPEC announced an increase in the price of oil from $2 US to $15 US per barrel, the impact was a decade-long stagflation (inflation with high unemployment; see next chapter). Canadian firms paid more for their oil, and income was redistributed from Canada to the OPEC countries. Since oil is used in the production of most goods, the higher price of oil caused production costs to rise. These were not absorbed by firms; had they been, there would have been little inflationary pressure. As prices increased dramatically, workers began losing ground as their real wages declined. To catch up, they demanded large wage increases, which only added fuel to the fire. The bottom line is that each group tried to shift the burden of higher energy costs onto others. The rest of the decade was caught in a wage-price/wage-wage spiral that culminated in the planned recession of 1980.

Wages should not be held solely accountable for inflation; the mark-up also plays a part. Once the firm knows all its production costs, the profit margin it chooses will depend on its intended investments and desired production level, as it will want to have access to continued final funding. While initial financing is a crucial component of investment, many economists prefer to emphasize the mark-up. One study shows that between 75 and 90 per cent of gross fixed capital expenditures in the United States manufacturing industry are financed through retained profits.[32] Thus, in essence, prices do not reflect the current demand conditions of the market, but the future needs of firms. It should be pointed out, however, that firms may not rely solely on prices to secure the necessary internal profits. Because a firm's income is determined both by prices and quantities, it may prefer to increase production.

Whether wages or the mark-up are more predominant in the pricing behaviour of firms is not so much the issue at hand. Both sources demonstrate the importance that income distribution plays in the economy; workers and producers attempt to keep their relative share of national income or gain a larger share, and are thus caught in a continual class struggle. This institutional approach is at the core of the real world, and must be reflected in any policy adopted to deal with inflation.

This theory of pricing behaviour is far more realistic and reasonable than the neoclassical supply-and-demand and money-supply theories. It assumes a realistic knowledge of the world in which firms operate and of the institutional forces at play, such as the distributional struggle between classes. In fact, "It is the maldistribution of wealth and the class struggle of society that determines prices, not supply and demand in competitive markets."[33]

Policy Implications: An Inflation Policy for the Real World

It is clear that the use of high interest rates and planned investments is a barbaric approach to fighting inflation. There is little doubt that it achieves its goals, although certainly not by ways determined by orthodox theory. By deliberately creating unemployment through the use of planned recessions, monetarists end up agreeing with Marx's claim that a "permanent army of unemployed" is needed to stabilize the capitalist market system. A high-interest-rate policy will affect inflation only if it has an impact on the wage-price spiral. In general, high interest rates will reduce investment and employment to the point that organized labour will not have the necessary clout to demand higher wages and fight over income distribution. In this context, firms will have less of an incentive to raise prices, especially since effective demand is low. This view is shared by post-Keynesian economists: government use "these instruments . . . to create enough unemployment to bring the trade unions to heel, and thereby bring the level of pay settlements sufficiently below the current rate of price inflation."[34]

Because inflation is not a monetary phenomenon, Keynes objected strongly to the use of a restrictive monetary policy or planned recessions to fight it, since no one has a vested interest in such policies except rentiers. He stated, "We must find other means of achieving this than a higher rate of interest. For if we allow the rate of interest to be affected, we cannot easily reverse the trend. . . . Thus it is a fatal mistake to use a high rate of interest as a means to dampen down the boom."[35] Furthermore, "The object of credit restriction . . . is to withdraw from employers the financial means to employ labour at the existing level of prices and wages. The policy can only attain its end by intensifying unemployment without limit, until the workers are ready to accept the necessary reduction of money wages under the pressure of hard facts. This is the so-called "sound" policy . . . from which any humane or judicious person must shrink."[36] Keynes believed that such a policy can only lead to increased speculative investments, as "ignorant" rentiers attempt to increase their own share of national income.

As stated above, neoclassical economists believe that any negative side effects of a high-interest-rate policy are temporary. However, there is no proof, as the current recession seems to indicate, that there is a "natural" tendency for the economy to correct itself. Every recent indicator seems to point to the contrary. Because the economy is path dependent, it may take years before Canada's economy is back on track.

Since inflation is neither a monetary or a fiscal phenomenon, it would appear useless to launch an attack based on these theoretical models (although this does not seem to have discouraged the federal government and the Bank of Canada from doing just that). If inflation is a social disagreement on the appropriate distribution of income, policies should reflect this. Therefore, it is not uncommon for post-Keynesians to advocate the use of an income policy or a productivity-geared wage policy to fight inflation. Such a policy would keep in mind the true nature of prices as an institutional and social phenomenon, independent of supply and demand and the scarcity of resources. Keynes noted that the "long-run stability or instability of prices will depend on the strength of the upward trend of the wage-unit . . . compared with the rate of increase in the efficiency of the productive system,"[37] where an incomes policy represents "psychological and political" considerations.

As such, wage increases could and should be made dependent on increases in productivity, measured perhaps at the national level. Of course, productive investments are the only credible way of guaranteeing increased productivity, since technical changes are "embodied" in new technology. A rejection of high interest rates and an increase in public investment would contribute significantly to capital accumulation and an increased standard of living for all.

Organized labour may criticize this approach as an infringement on its freedom to negotiate wage settlements. The problem with this view is that in the absence of an incomes policy, the consequences are more severe, and the classes will continue to fight over the appropriate distribution of income. Different groups must keep in mind the over-all goal, which is price stability and a more equitable distribution of income and wealth. In this context, the means justify the end, to paraphrase Machiavelli.

An incomes policy is very different from a programme of wage and price controls. In essence, while controls are imposed upon workers and firms, an incomes policy should—and must—be voluntary; otherwise, there is no use for it. Such a policy is designed to obtain a "social agreement among domestic competing groups to limit their demands for real income in a manner which is socially responsible for distributing the remaining GNP and hence limiting current inflation."[38]

The alternative to an incomes policy is the current situation and policies. Those who are opposed to an incomes policy would do best to keep in mind that the hardships of economic cycles—permanent high unemployment and reduced real income—are only some of the consequences of the current high-interest-rate policy; a reduced capital stock and poor private-sector productivity will also result.

Of course, an incomes policy should not be put in place in the absence of other institutional policies, because it revolves around the concept of a social agreement between all concerned. Nonetheless, it would be a definite step toward reducing inflation and the present unequitable distribution of income. What is needed is the political and social will to increase the well-being of society as a whole so that all groups within it can increase their total wealth without having to fear eventual restrictive policies that serve no one but the rentiers.

Notes

1. Of monetarists, Nicholas Kaldor once wrote, "The distinguishing mark of this new wave of monetarism is its dogmatism and complete lack of intellectual coherence." See Kaldor, *The Scourge of Monetarism*, p. xxii.
2. Quoted in Appelbaum, "The Labor Market," p. 35.
3. Friedman and Schwartz, *A Monetary History*. For a critical analysis of Friedman's work, see Russel, *Fallacies of Monetarism*.
4. M. Friedman, "A Theoretical Framework," p. 27.
5. Keynes, *Collected Writings*, vol. 13, p. 409.
6. Tobin, "Theoretical Issues in Macroeconomics," pp. 108–9.
7. Kaldor likened this analogy to an "aerial Santa Claus." See Kaldor, *The Scourge of Monetarism*, p. 28.
8. Seccareccia, *Post-Keynesian Fundism*, p. 1.
9. Lavoie, *Foundations of Post-Keynesian*, p. 153
10. Moore, "The Endogeneity of Money," p. 399.
11. Keynes, *Collected Writings*, vol. 27, p. 390.
12. Dutt, "Rentiers in Post-Keynesian Models," p. 98.
13. Kaldor, *The Scrourge of Monetarism*, p. 47.
14. Eichner, *Macrodynamics of Advanced.*
15. Keynes, *Collected Writings*, pp. 218, 228, 229. Kaldor claimed that *The Consequences of Mr. Churchill*, reprinted in vol. 9 of the *Collected Writings*, pp. 207–29, was "ahead of its time and ahead of much of Keynes's own writing on the subject." Kaldor, *The Scourge of Monetarism*, p. xx.
16. Quoted in Lavoie, *Foundations of Post-Keynesian*, p. 187. See also Kaldor, *The Scourge of Monetarism*.

17. Moore, *Horizontalists*, pp. 3–4. For empirical results, see Shannon and Wallace, "Wages and Inflation."
18. Lavoie, *Foundations of Post-Keynesian*, p. 216.
19. In neoclassical theory, demand would rise because of an oversupply of money.
20. Cripps, "The Money Supply," p. 110.
21. Marshall, *Principles of Economics*, p. 461.
22. Kenyon, "Pricing," p. 34.
23. Means, "The Administered-Price Thesis Reconfirmed," pp. 292–3.
24. Hicks, *The Crisis in Keynesian Economics*, p. 78.
25. Lavoie, *Foundations of Post-Keynesian*, p. 386.
26. Davidson, *Money and the Real World*.
27. Lavoie, *Foundations of Post-Keynesian*, p. 377.
28. Davidson, "Post Keynesian Economics," p. 163.
29. For more on this subject, see Koutsoyiannis, *Modern Microeconomics*.
30. Sawyer, *The Challenge of Radical Political Economy*, p. 363.
31. Keynes, *Collected Writings*, vol. 7, p. 14.
32. Eichner, *The Megacorp and the Oligopoly*.
33. Rousseas, *Post Keynesian Monetary Economics*, p. 9.
34. See Kaldor, *The Scourge of Monetarism*, p. 55.
35. Keynes, *Collected Writings*, vol. 21, p. 389.
36. Ibid., vol. 11, p. 218.
37. Ibid., vol. 12, p. 309.
38. Davidson, "Post Keynesian Economics," p. 163.

CHAPTER FIVE

UNEMPLOYMENT: FICTION VERSUS REALITY

If heterodox economists have for years ignored, or at least put aside, worries concerning inflation and its policy implications, the same cannot be said about unemployment. While Keynes was concerned with both phenomena, it is unemployment that has been at the forefront of "Keynesian" macro-economic policies for most of the postwar years. In a sense, there was perhaps less of a need to fight inflation in light of the unemployment crisis of the 1930s and 1940s and subsequent periods of unemployment. "Keynesian" policies that were later developed and applied were based largely on the unemployment aspect of Keynes's *General Theory*. As we have seen, Keynes had much to say about the question of inflation, which he carefully linked to the issue of employment and wages. It is therefore difficult, within the context in which Keynes developed his theory, to separate the two.

Unemployment is not only an economic problem, but a social one as well, inasmuch as its consequences are not limited to any one individual. As unemployment persists, employed workers run the risk of losing their jobs, as has been made clear in recent recessions, especially the current one. Unemployment acts as a drain on the economy, siphoning off great human capital potential. In this light, unemployment must be seen as the greatest failure of modern capitalist economies. It is astonishing to witness the nonchalance of so many politicians—and economists—with regard to this issue. It is both socially intolerable and politically and economically unacceptable. One Canadian economist, Jack Weldon, expressed his anger toward this indifference: "In what imaginary world do these economists live who calmly believe that the loss of a few thousand actual jobs is a small price to pay for their 'pledge of faith.'"[1]

Weldon is referring to the social dimension of unemployment. The loss of a job is not a personal choice, as many economists still like to believe, but a result of forces beyond the control of workers. The very concept of unemployment insurance implies that as a society, we have accepted the responsibility for the misfortunes of others, and the expression "no fault of their own" has come to symbolize the idea that the causes of unemployment are rooted in the nature of a monetary capitalist economy of production, not in individual choices and preferences. Unemployment is not a "normal" phenomenon, but the result of deliberate economic policies. As such, it can be corrected only through economic and activist policies.

The need to work is perceived to be one of the most important dimensions of human life. Work—or, at least, the income we get from work—allows us to pursue financial, intellectual, and physical independence, and enables us to become full participants in society.

Neoclassical Theory and Voluntary Unemployment

It is difficult to escape the neoclassical analysis of supply and demand; it is, within the body of orthodox theory, a universal law that determines simultaneously the price and the quantity of every commodity, including labour, in its respective market. This implies that labour forms a market of its own, in which supply and demand determine its price—the real wage rate—and its quantity—the level of employment. Thus, labour is considered a commodity among many others.

There are some supposedly simple and obvious assumptions within the neoclassical labour theory that merit special attention, for they underlie Canada's current approach to economic policy with regard to unemployment. This neoconservative approach was also the cornerstone of the 1986 Macdonald Royal Commission, many of whose recommendations were implemented by the federal government.

The Supply of Labour

The mainstream analysis of labour supply rests on the notion that workers, given a twenty-four-hour day, must decide whether they wish to consume leisure or work. Since work gives them wage income with which to purchase other goods and services, the choice is between the consumption of leisure or of other goods. The entire day is so divided. Hours spent working are hours in which workers cannot enjoy leisure; in this sense, work is a sacrifice for which workers must be compensated, and it therefore carries with it a certain degree of disutility (dissatisfaction). Furthermore, the objective of workers is to maximize their well-being, so they must carefully consider what quantity of work and what quantity of leisure they will consume. At a given wage rate, no workers are willing to increase the hours spent working, since this new combination of work and leisure will not maximize their well-being; it would be worthwhile only if the wage rate were increased. Workers therefore voluntarily offer their services. The individual supply of labour is thus positively related to the real wage; when it goes up, so does the quantity supplied, as workers see this as a more profitable situation.

The concept of the supply of labour depends on a most important component: the real wage, defined as the nominal wage divided by prices. It is assumed, in neoclassical theory, that workers are most concerned with the real wage rate, although they are paid in nominal wages. It is further assumed that workers possess the ability and the necessary information to translate their nominal wages into real wages, and that they are capable of immediately calculating the full effect of price-level changes on purchasing power. As prices increase, real wages decrease. The aggregate quantity of labour supplied by all workers in the economy is obtained simply by adding up individual supply curves. It is also positively correlated with the real wage.

The Demand for Labour

In discussing the neoclassical analysis of the demand for labour, it is important to remember that the only objective of the firm is profit maximization, and any decision to hire labour is based on this goal. A firm will hire workers, but will pay them only the equivalent of their contribution to production—their marginal product. After all, why would a firm pay workers ten dollars an hour if they contribute only eight dollars' worth to production? It is assumed that, given a fixed quantity of capital stock, each additional labourer contributes less and less to production. One can imagine a factory with one large machine. If one person operates it, he can produce 100 goods; his contribution is 100. However, as workers are added to the production process, total production might increase, but at a decreasing rate. The second worker might help raise production to 150, but his contribution is only 50, which is much less than the first worker's. This is referred to as the law of decreasing marginal product of labour, and it dictates the demand for labour. Firms will hire additional workers only if the real wage rate decreases, so that the quantity demanded and the real wage rate are negatively related. Labour will be hired until the value of the output produced by the last worker employed just equals the wage paid.

The Labour Market

Within neoclassical economics, a market exists for labour, as it does for other commodities. In this labour market, supply and demand interact to determine the equilibrium real wage rate and level of employment. The wage rate is a market clearing price, in which quantity supplied equals quantity demanded. It adjusts to any changes that develop in the market in order to guarantee equilibrium. The Smithian self-regulatory mechanisms are in place, and market forces are capable of guaranteeing full employment. Government policies are therefore not necessary, and may even prove to be harmful.

All the scenarios associated with neoclassical supply-and-demand analysis are applicable in this market as well. Unemployment is therefore explained exclusively through labour-market forces—the result of an oversupply or a deficient demand, both the result of too high real wages. As the real wage increases, it induces more workers to join the labour force (oversupply) and forces firms to cut back employment. If wages are allowed to come down, and if workers are prepared to accept these lower wages, unemployment will disappear.

The process restoring equilibrium is automatic and rapid, because nominal wages are flexible. Unemployment is seen as a voluntary phenomenon; if it persists, it is because workers are unwilling to work at lower wages. Neoclassical economists have in fact explained the persistence of high unemployment in the last two decades by a number of "institutional" factors that have prevented nominal wages from coming down to their more "natural" levels. For example, laws such as those setting the minimum wage cause unemployment, since workers are not "worth" that much. Unions also prevent nominal wages from adjusting downward, therefore contributing to unemployment. Finally, the high unemployment of the 1970s was blamed on women and baby-boomers, who, as they were enticed or of age to enter the labour market, created an oversupply of labour. Nominal wages did not adjust downward, leading to persistent high unemployment.

The Smithian process of market clearing is believed to be instantaneous. In the previous chapter, it was noted that neoclassical economists and monetarists believe that a restrictive monetary policy would have no effect on the "real" economy, and that in the long run employment levels would not be affected. The mechanics of this *laissez-faire* approach are simplistically unrealistic. Assuming that the Bank of Canada has control over the supply of money, and that it adopts a restrictive policy, the interest rate will be pushed up. As the growth of the money supply is reduced, it is assumed, the general price level will follow, causing the real wage of workers to rise; this leads to an increased supply, a reduced demand, and, consequently, unemployment. That is in the short run. In the long run (the duration of which is not defined), the excess supply of labour would exert downward pressure on nominal wages, which are assumed to be flexible. In turn, real wages would return to their original level. As a result, employment would rise to its original equilibrium, full-employment level. Both the real and the nominal wage rates are hence determined within the labour market: the economy triumphs, since prices are lower. And what about higher interest rates? Neoclassical theory stipulates that since nominal wages and prices are reduced, households have less of a need to hold money for day-to-day transactions. Households (and firms) would then choose to buy bonds, pushing up their price and, as a result, lowering the interest rate. And everybody lives happily ever after.

Wages serve another function in neoclassical theory: they act as the market's way of redistributing income among workers. In this context, as opposed to the heterodox approach described in the previous chapter, distribution need not be equitable, just efficient. All workers receive the income they deserve based on their contribution to the production process.

It is clear that this is not what is presently happening in the real world. Neoclassical theory refuses to deal with institutions, such as trade unions, and with the inherently unstable and uncertain nature of capitalist economies. Before turning to an alternative view of the labour market, let us first have a look at another theory that has developed over the years since the publication of Keynes's *General Theory*.

Unemployment and Inflation: Trade-Off or Myth?

In the 1950s, two American economists, Paul Samuelson and Robert Solow, became interested in the possible links between variations in the unemployment rate and the rate of inflation. Encouraged by an empirical study by British economist A.W. Phillips,[2] Samuelson and Solow examined the relationship between unemployment and the "annual wage inflation rate" in the postwar American economy. Their research led to an abundant literature, which convinced politicians of all stripes that there is a stable inverse relationship between unemployment and inflation. Politicians and policy makers were therefore limited in their choice of fiscal policy. If they attempted to reduce unemployment through expansionary fiscal policies, they would inevitably let loose inflationary pressures.

This relationship between unemployment and inflation, known as the Phillips curve, remains standard teaching in introductory economics courses, and most textbooks continue to give it prominent treatment. The idea is still very popular among politicians, who argue that "a little unemployment" is needed to guarantee price stability.

The conventional Phillips analysis of inflation rests on three basic postulates: that wages are determined exclusively by market forces; that increases in employment are necessarily inflationary; and that inflation is demand-determined. Although many economists claim that the Phillips curve is a "Keynesian" model, it should be clear that this is not so. Keynes rejected all three of these postulates, and there is nothing in the *General Theory* to suggest that such a relationship exists. In fact, it could just as easily be argued that the Phillips curve is more neoclassical in nature.

Although the Phillips curve is based on three central neoclassical assumptions, orthodox economists reject the analysis, and point rather to the events of the late 1960s and early 1970s to show that the relationship is weak, or even nonexistent. In 1976, Milton Friedman established precisely that the simultaneous presence of high inflation and unemployment seemed to contradict the notion that there was a trade-off between the two. Friedman concluded that economists should therefore look elsewhere if they wanted to understand the causes of inflation (Friedman's "monetary phenomenon" theory). Advocates of the Phillips curve, however, concluded that the relationship still existed, although the curve itself had shifted upward. The spirited debate over these apparently contradictory views has dominated economic literature in the last twenty years. Unable to explain the simultaneous presence of high inflation and high unemployment in the 1970s, the Phillips curve analysis ultimately contributed to the demise of "bastard" Keynesianism.

Unemployment and the Real World: An Alternative

As we have seen above, many economists reject the view that price stability and full employment are necessarily irreconcilable objectives. Neoclassical economists and "bastard Keynesians" attribute persistent unemployment to the existence of rigid nominal wages, which, due to powerful unions, are not allowed to decline to their "natural" level. A great majority of economists are of the opinion that Keynes defended this notion of wage "stickiness." Nothing could be further from the truth. Although it is true that Keynes used rigid wages in his formal model in the *General Theory*, he also believed that flexible wages would not, and could not, guarantee full employment.[3] When he later dropped the rigid-wage postulate, he still concluded that nominal wage flexibility was not a sufficient condition for full employment.

In Keynes's view, automatic wage mechanisms do not exist. In fact, he believed that real and nominal (or money) wages are subject to two different sets of influences, and may even move in opposite directions. Money wages depend primarily on the bargaining strength of organized labour, while real wages are determined by prices. As I have pointed out, prices reflect the market or monopoly power of firms, as well as their need for internal funding. Real wages are therefore a factor of economic activity and planned investments, and are primarily a redistributive variable.

Keynes also questioned whether flexible money wages were in fact desirable. Consider for a moment the impact of a generalized decrease in nominal wages. Since firms' proceeds depend on the sale of their commodities, lowering nominal wages would reduce effective demand—that is, the amount of money that is spent on consumption. As firms sell less, they have less of a need to continue production at the same level, and will most likely start laying off workers, perpetuating the situation. In this sense, it is a good thing that workers resist reductions in nominal wages. Keynes sardonically remarked that it was "quite fortunate that the workers, though unconsciously, are instinctively more reasonable economists than the [neo]classical school, inasmuch as they resist reductions in money-wages."[4] In addition, flexible wages would subject firms to a great deal of uncertainty. Imagine how firms would react if they ignored not only the amplitude but also the direction of any future changes in nominal wages. By installing some degree of stability and by reducing uncertainty, rigid money wages (as well as administered prices) make planning less difficult, allowing firms to carry out the production process and to adopt a longer-run view of investments.

The "Labour Market"

Keynes did not see the validity of neoclassical supply-and-demand analysis within the context of the labour "market." "The concept of a 'labour market' in which the supposed fundamental relations of supply and demand interact to determine the 'price of labour' and its quantity is totally alien to both Keynes's and post-Keynesian thinking on the matter."[5] In fact, such a market does not properly exist: wages are not "just another price," and workers are not commodities. The price and quantity of labour supplied depend on variables and forces outside this so-called market, and are determined by two separate set of forces.

Unlike other goods, labour has particular properties to which it is difficult to apply any sort of supply-and-demand analysis. First of all, labour cannot be stored and is perishable; if it is not used now, it is "lost forever." Furthermore, "labour power" cannot be disassociated from workers, and if their skills, knowledge, and productivity are not used, they will generally tend to diminish. Finally, when they enter the labour market, workers bring with them their whole "past history and norms of justice,"[6] unlike commodities in other markets. For these reasons, among others, this approach to labour-market theory has been called "anthropogenic" because "it focuses on the cumulative acquisition of competence over time"[7] due to affiliations with specific classes and institutions, families, and schooling.

As with price formation, the labour market is divided into two sub-markets, in a theory referred to as the "dual economy." Each segment has very different characteristics. The primary, or core, economy corresponds to the sectors or markets in which prices are largely administered by oligopolies and monopolies. It is characterized by low fluctuations or variations in demand, a high capital-to-labour ratio, a greater demand for skilled workers, high money wages with low variance, high productivity, and a relatively unionized workforce. As well, firms have a greater tendency to develop a more stable attachment to or affiliation with their workers, mainly through a highly hierarchical wage structure in which experience and seniority are prominent features.

The secondary, or peripheral, segment is largely dominated by smaller, more competitive firms, processes, and structures, and more labour-intensive production techniques. Labour training is less important and nominal wages are significantly lower, although there is a greater variance among workers' wages. This segment commonly includes the "service" sector.

Labour Supply: An Alternative View

Keynes's attack on the supply of labour relates to the idea that workers do not increase or withdraw their labour with changes in the price level. After all, they have a number of financial obligations that they must meet, and work, for most labourers, is their only source of income. Necessity and the lack of alternatives force them to offer their services despite declining real wages. Work is also a source of self-respect and contributes to workers' sense of self-worth; it is not only disutility, but can also be rewarding. Workers are therefore not in a position to withdraw their services simply because real wages may not be at a "satisfactory" level. Historically, there have been significant changes in the level of employment unrelated to changes in the level of real wages. In its twenty-sixth annual report, the now-defunct Economic Council of Canada (1989) concluded that real wages in Canada have been decreasing over the last twenty years. Since this is the case, why has the unemployment rate continued to move steadily upward? Why have wages not played their market-clearing function?

Empirical studies have shown that in many instances, the general composition of the supply of labour is quite at odds with the traditional view that real wages are negatively correlated with hours of work. If the real wage were to decrease, workers would be willing to offer more hours of work, contrary to neoclassical theory, which sees work as a "voluntary" phenomenon. One reason for this is that as wages decrease, workers want to compensate their loss of income by working additional hours. In this context, the decision or need to work cannot be separated from the need for consumption; moreover, households' financial responsibilities and contractual obligations compel them to maintain the level of income to which they have become accustomed. Simply put, workers will want to keep up with their past consumption levels.

A second reason may be workers' desire to maintain their relative standing in society and their community. The individual supply of labour can thus be said to depend on the "normal standard of living of a household *relative* to that of other households."[8] All in all, the supply of labour can said to be based on the "keeping up with the Joneses" syndrome.

Despite these findings, many heterodox economists are reluctant to use this new labour-supply curve in any supply-and-demand analysis. The fact that the reasons for workers' decisions to offer their services are far from those described by neoclassical theory does not alter the view that pure market forces determine employment and wages. It would still come down to supply and demand.

The desire to maintain a certain standard of living tells us very little about how particular workers are siphoned into the core and peripheral segments of the labour market. Many heterodox econo-mists share the view that individuals are moulded by their social and institutional surroundings—that they are a product, so to speak, of their environments. Workers are integrated into the labour force through a multi-step process of affiliations, starting with the family and continuing through life with school and a circle of friends. "The choice of the ultimate affiliation in the workplace [is not] inde-pendent of the other social affiliations, with the effect being that career paths are highly compartmentalized and dependent upon the social milieu that originally moulded the individual partici-pant."[9] Social and class barriers prevent individuals from having the luxury of freely making career decisions. Peanut farmers who become presidents, for instance, are the exception, not the norm. In the real world, individuals are often caught in cycles that are difficult to escape, and that often determine whether they end up in core or peripheral industries. Thus, a household's "normal standard of living" will, in all likelihood, be dictated by its social affiliation and milieu.

The Determination of Wages

This issue was discussed at length in the previous chapter; here, it suffices to say that Keynes was mostly concerned with the workings of a monetary production economy in which contracts, including wages, are expressed in terms of money. As he set forth in the *General Theory*, Keynes did not believe that wages were related to workers' contribution to production, but rather to forces outside the labour market. In collective bargaining, the primary concern of all workers is to protect their standing in comparison to other workers—that is, their relative nominal wages. As he pointed out, "The struggle about money-wages primarily affects the *distribution* of the aggregate real wage between different labour-groups."[10] The importance of the so-called sociological factors—historical and social norms—cannot be overlooked as workers adapt to the norms and role patterns of the work group in which they exist. "Although custom has never achieved a place in the formal analytical apparatus of economics, its role in wage determination has been recognized by virtually every student of the labor market from Adam Smith to J. R. Hicks."[11] Social policies such as "equal pay for work of equal value," although desirable from an income-distribution point of view, would upset the traditional ranking of labour groups within society; as well, the likely result, a wage-wage spiral, would probably prove inflationary. Collective bargaining and nominal wage determination are often based on nominal wage increases of other groups. For example, police officers might want to have the same nominal increase as that of fire fighters, so that the "gap"—if there is one—remains the same. One example of the strong resistance to changes in wage relativity was when New York mayor Ed Koch rejected an advisory panel's recommendation that police officers' pay be increased by 42 per cent. "Attempts to change relative wage rates in the 1960s [had] proved to be unsuccessful, and very costly to the city as firemen (and other workers) were able to regain parity (or their traditional ratio) with police officers' pay at higher levels."[12]

The aggregate level of money wages is therefore determined by a set of factors within a historical context. It could be argued that at any point in time, the level of nominal wages is a historical accident[13] "regulated by exogenous sociopolitical forces that have worked themselves out in the past . . . [in which] the relationship between employers and current employees is an ongoing one,"[14] while real wages are an income-distribution variable between workers and entrepreneurs.

The Demand for Labour

In the real world, the level of employment is determined exclusively by the demand for labour. Unlike neoclassical theory, in which the interaction of supply and demand determine employment, in the real world, firms hire labour no matter what the level of supply is; that is, "the volume of labour forthcoming at a given wage depends on the availability of jobs."[15] Firms therefore have a definite advantage over labour, because they can determine the appropriate level of jobs at any given wage rate. In other words, supply is dependent on demand. If, for instance, firms suddenly decided collectively to offer thousands of jobs, the supply of labour would adjust quickly enough, as people would be encouraged to join the labour force.

This alternative approach to labour-market policies has been developed in an attempt to embody the reality of institutions and their role in determining or influencing the demand for labour. It is perhaps this part of the theory that is the most at odds with neoclassical theory. Mainstream economists approach labour demand from a very consistent and mathematical perspective, in which the level of demand is strictly determined by real wages, while heterodox economists see the relationship as strictly positive—increases in wages will lead to increases in employment.

If entrepreneurs are more concerned with increasing the growth of their firm or their share of the market than with maximizing profits, firms' level of production and investment will be more important. To produce more, firms must first hire additional labour; hence, the demand for labour increases. Similarly, if they acquire additional capital stock, they will need more labour to operate the equipment. It was central to Keynes's philosophy that the level of output and employment as a whole depends on the amount of investment. However, investment is prone to extreme fluctuations because of the uncertainty upon which it is based.

For Keynes, uncertainty was the single most important aspect of modern capitalism. Neoclassical economists ignore the existence of uncertainty, perhaps because it does not fit well within their theory, or because it is not quantifiable, and turn instead to risk, believing that it is a close approximation; however, the two concepts are not at all the same. Whereas risk can be measured, uncertainty cannot. A pioneering work on risk states, "The practical difference between the two categories, risk and uncertainty, is that in the former the distribution of the outcome in a group of instances is known (either through calculation *a priori* or from statistics of past experience), while in the case of uncertainty this is not true, the reason being in general that it is impossible to form a group of instances, because the situation dealt with is in a high degree unique."[16] Risk therefore implies a situation in which all possible outcomes are known with certainty, as are the probabilities associated with each outcome. For instance, lotteries are a game of risk. There is nothing uncertain about them. Holders of a lottery ticket know that they may have a 10 per cent chance of winning, say, $10,000, while they have a 90 per cent chance of not winning anything at all. Buying a ticket is risky, but there is no uncertainty involved. In this example, uncertainty would be a situation in which an individual buys a lottery ticket but has no knowledge of the amount of money that could be won, nor of the probabilities. It would simply be a shot in the dark. Hence, the uncertainty that surrounds the outcome of decisions in economic and political life cannot be reduced to calculable risks by applying the concepts of mathematical probability.

We often hear that investments can be "risky," but this is an error in vocabulary. Investment is not risky. Firms and entrepreneurs have no knowledge of possible outcomes, possible returns on their investment, or the probabilities associated with each outcome. Indeed, investment faces an uncertain future and is quite volatile.

Economic theory must therefore deal with uncertainty, as decision makers, households, firms, and governments move away from an irreversible past. Uncertainty is inevitable when economists choose to deal with the reality of calendar time. As I explained in chapter one, Keynes's theory was set in what economists call "historical time," in which decisions made in the past affect the present, and decisions made today are very much dependent on the unknown future. More precisely, investment decisions taken in the past affect a firm's current production capacity, while investment decisions taken today are based on long-term expectations of the future direction and amplitude of economic performance. The passage of time between decisions and outcome is a fundamental fact. The time between the decision to produce, the investment, the appearance of a product, and the revenues generated from its sales is likely to stretch over many weeks, months, or years. A plant cannot be built overnight, nor can labour be hired and trained in a day. The benefits from any type of investment or decision to raise production are therefore dependent on far-reaching, forward-looking expectations, and will occur long after the commitment to action has been undertaken. Our knowledge about the economy is thus asymmetrical: we know the past but not the future.

This prompted Keynes to refer to neoclassical theory as "one of those pretty polite techniques which tries to deal with the present by abstracting from the fact that we know very little about the future."[17] The attempt to ignore uncertainty is a grave mistake, for it greatly affects the level of investments in the economy. Since increased production and investment lead to increased demand for labour, employment can be said to depend on expectations of future events. To understand the causes of economic cycles—periods of prosperity and recessions/depressions—we must therefore understand how uncertainty affects investments. Keynes and post-Keynesians imply that productive investment is the source of economic growth. The question pertinent to understanding unemployment is the following: What makes a firm decide to invest rather than retain a liquid position?

For Keynes, since the future is by definition unknown, investments can at best depend on some sort of rule of thumb—on entrepreneurs' optimism or pessimism, based on emotions and an entrepreneurial culture, rather than a precise calculation. "There is the instability due to the characteristic of human nature that a large portion of our positive activities depend on a *spontaneous* optimism rather than a mathematical expectation. . . . Most probably, of our decisions to do something positive, the full consequences of which will be drawn out over very many days to come, can only be taken as the result of *animal spirits*—a spontaneous urge to action rather than inaction."[18] Furthermore, firms that are more optimistic will be at a distinct disadvantage. Economic growth is the result not of the investments of a single firm, but of a certain collective conscience. If one firm decides to increase its production while others are reluctant to do so, it will not be able to sell its goods, since effective demand will be low and the aggregate level of income will not have been affected. This has obvious consequences on the level of employment at any point in time:

> The decision to produce and to hire labour is not, in a market economy, a collective decision but rather an individual one. However, the individual entrepreneur will not be able to increase production of his product unless other entrepreneurs simultaneously increase their production (by increasing the global level of wages and thus of aggregate demand). . . . In a capitalist system, therefore, the entrepreneur whose "animal spirits" are more optimistic than others is necessarily penalized. While the overall interest is for all entrepreneurs to have the highest "animal spirits," the interest of a single entrepreneur is best served when his own optimism is not more so than others.[19]

Furthermore, "Any one firm, acting in isolation, may find that the market for its own products is limited, and will therefore refrain from expanding its production. . . . If all firms acted in collusion, in *all* industries, it would be a different matter, since the increased output of all firms would increase the demand for every one of them sufficiently to justify the increased output. But in the absence of such coordinated action the system can be in equilibrium at *any* level of employment and output."[20]

The role that "animal spirits" play is a crucial one, as entrepreneurs' feelings about the uncertain future can change greatly. However, it should not be forgotten that while optimism and pessimism are key elements, entrepreneurs' decisions are also based on more rational behaviour, as Keynes also noted. "We should not conclude from this that everything depends on waves of irrational psychology. . . . We are merely reminding ourselves that human decisions affecting the future, whether personal or political or economic, cannot depend on strict mathematical expectation, since the basis for making such calculation does not exist; and that it is our innate urge to activity which makes the wheels go round."[21]

While expectations with respect to future events are important, we must distinguish, as Keynes did, between two types of expectations: short term and long term, each with very different consequences. Production decisions at any given point in time (and therefore employment levels) are said to be dependent on expectations of the near future. The relevant question to entrepreneurs is whether increased production, through an increase in the degree of utilization, will be met by additional sales. Therefore, the decision to increase production is based on the short-term expectation of prices at the time of the sale of the output: "The entrepreneur . . . has to form the best expectations he can as to what the consumers will be prepared to pay when he is ready to supply them . . . and he has no choice but to be guided by those expectations if he is to produce at all."[22] Market prices of goods are not determined before production, and there is no guarantee that prices will be those expected by entrepreneurs: "Actual prices are only relevant for production decisions insofar as they influence expectations."[23] Therefore, since firms always operate at less than full capacity, they have the flexibility to respond to changes in demand. Firms will ordinarily respond not by raising prices, but by increasing production. To produce more, they must hire additional labour. In the short term, therefore, labour demand will be based on the degree of utilization of firms, not on the real wage.

Long-term expectations affect entrepreneurs' decisions to invest and increase their capital stock, as they are concerned with the possible, though uncertain, patterns of future returns or quasi-rents to be earned over the life of the investments in capital equipment. It is the potential variability and unreliability of these expectations that led Keynes to identify investment as the *causa causans* of his system. Long-period expectations are the most important element in determining investments. Interest rates are also a factor, but to a lesser degree; a fall in the interest rate would stimulate investments, but only by making investment financing easier.

Faced with an uncertain future, entrepreneurs rely on conventions and norms, often using the past or the present to guide themselves through difficult decisions. For example, a survey that shows consumer confidence at record lows is not an encouraging sign for entrepreneurs. So the present does enter into the equation, although indirectly, as there is no guarantee of its stability. As Keynes noted, "The facts of the existing situation enter, in a sense disproportionately, into the formation of our long-term expectations."[24]

There is another important aspect to this theory: consumption. Firms must be able to sell their production. Whether based on short-term or long-term expectations, the level of effective demand will determine, over all, the direction of production and investment. After all, if a firm does not expect its product to sell, it has very little incentive to increase production or capital stock. Employment and the economy as a whole are therefore not constrained by scarcity but by demand. The economy can be said to be a vicious circle. Higher effective demand from lower unemployment would instill confidence in the economy. To reduce unemployment, however, investments must increase. It is a catch-22 situation. With the economy stuck in a situation of less than full employment, Keynes saw the state as playing a vital role in "socializing" investment, thereby increasing effective demand.

Keynes believed that only when economists understand how a "general theory" of a monetary production economy operates can they give useful policy advice. Policy makers could then be pressured to take positive actions to eliminate unemployment, rather than waiting for long-run free-market forces to move the economy toward a natural full-employment level.

By the above arguments, it should be clear that unemployment is not a personal choice, but a result of the economic system. If firms do not choose to hire additional labour, it is because they have little confidence in the market's capacity to generate sufficient demand.

Full Employment

Although all economists agree on the fundamental importance of full employment and perceive it as a desirable goal, neoclassical economists and post-Keynesians greatly disagree on what constitutes an acceptable level of full employment and on the proper policies to achieve it.

Historically, both in Canada and abroad, there have been many definitions of full employment. Although it may be easy to describe, it is difficult to define in terms that are sufficiently precise to generate consensus. Many economists have defined full employment along statistical lines, ranging anywhere from 3 per cent unemployment (as defined by the Economic Council of Canada in the 1960s) to 8 per cent or even 9 per cent. Other economists, believing in a certain trade-off between unemployment and inflation, talk about a "natural" rate of unemployment or a level of employment that would not lead to inflationary pressures, a "nonaccelerating inflation rate of unemployment." As stated above, there are no significant empirical studies that have clearly demonstrated this argument. In fact, in 1986, two separate committees of the Organization for Economic Co-operation and Development concluded that such a trade-off does not exist in the real world.[25]

The rise of monetarism and its barbaric economic policies in recent years have contributed to the exclusion of the term "full employment" from the vocabulary of mainstream economics.[26] When was the last time we heard politicians speak of a full-employment policy? The sad truth is that it has been decades.

Other economists describe full employment as a situation in which anyone who is willing to work is given the opportunity. This would amount to a commitment to eliminating involuntary unemployment. Many, including advocates of the natural-rate hypothesis, believe that such a definition would automatically lead to inflation. However, as was explained in the previous chapter, inflation is primarily a question of rising wages. This does not mean that full employment could not lead to higher wages, although,

132

without the proper institutional policies, this may indeed be the case. As Keynes noted, in good times, when firms' proceeds are rising, organized labour may have more influence and could win concessions during collective bargaining; furthermore, entrepreneurs may be more willing to meet labour's demands. This has led many heterodox economists to speak of a full-employment policy within the larger context of an incomes policy. Keynes believed that this was perhaps the most important obstacle to full employment. "If money wages rise faster than efficiency, this aggravates the difficulty of maintaining full employment, and, so far from being a condition for full employment, it is one of the main obstacles which a full employment policy has to overcome."[27] He therefore emphasized the importance of tying wage increases to productivity gains.

The next logical question is, How can we achieve full employment? It should be obvious that if left to itself, the market is not capable of guaranteeing full employment. Heterodox economists have therefore developed and promoted two approaches that are not necessarily mutually exclusive. The first is the tripartite approach, a partnership between government, business, and labour; the second is an income-distribution approach combined with planned investment. Either way, full employment must be seen as both a social and an economic policy.

While the idea of partnership is much discussed currently, there are certain aspects that must be emphasized. What I propose is not a partnership to resolve inflation through cost-cutting measures, or a quasi-crypto-partnership in which labour is merely a pawn wielding no significant power or influence. Many academics have claimed that a tripartite system is needed more today than at any time in our history, because the rise of economic interventionism in recent decades has created a highly complex infrastructure within capitalist economies and interdependent links between economic actors with multiple and far-reaching ramifications. This interdependence can be a blessing as well as a curse. At the very least, it brings into question the effectiveness of government policies: without the co-operation of labour and business, how success-ful can such policies be? Today, it has reached the point that it has become difficult to identify exactly where the influence of a particular group begins and ends.

Could a tripartite system work in Canada? Under the present conditions, I doubt that it could. However, with the proper institu-tional mechanisms in place, it could work well, as it does in other countries; we would, of course, need to adopt a structure that fits our needs. We might even have to consider a major restructuring of the way labour movements operate.

Within an alternative context, partnership clearly means that labour has the same weight as business and government in any decision-making body. (Whether government and business would accept such a transfer of power is unknown.) The objective would be to replace the somewhat imperfect market forces with a series of consensual agreements. "The adoption of a *permanent* incomes policy may be the best longer-term solution, but it requires com-plex new institutional arrangements to replace the prevailing sys-tems of wage bargaining; it requires far-reaching consensus and co-operation by the three 'social partners,' Capital, Labour, and Government."[28]

A tripartite structure also means an agreement on fighting unem-ployment first, and on adopting policies that may help achieve this goal. I have elsewhere discussed the advantages—and disadvan-tages—of such a social agreement, given the inherently antagonis-tic nature of labour-management-government relations, especially in recent years.[29] Attempts have been made in the past, but their relative failure cannot be a good sign, since they were not a truly equitable partnership to begin with. Nonetheless, the advantages seem to be quite interesting. Many studies[30] have shown that countries in which such a tripartite structure is in place have experienced greater economic growth, lower unemployment, lower inflation, and a greater degree of "social peace." They have also generally fared better during recessions, and even during the oil crisis of the 1970s.

Those who are skeptical of the successes of a tripartite system should take note that many nineteenth-century theorists thought that the simultaneous existence of a capitalist economy and a democratic political structure based on universal suffrage could only lead to disaster. Marx believed that it would lead to the demise and fall of the bourgeoisie, while Mill and de Tocqueville were convinced that it would result in the despotism of the majority. Of course, history has disproved each apocalyptic scenarios.

Even though a consensual approach is a realistic and useful objective, there is another approach, which, indeed, could include an implicit assumption of the tripartite formula: income redistribution. Non-mainstream economists are particularly concerned with the question of income distribution among groups in society. Inevitably, how income is distributed between classes—workers, entrepreneurs, and rentiers—will affect the level of employment in the economy due to their respective propensities to save.

Since growth of the economy is constrained by demand, if income is redistributed from workers to entrepreneurs and rentiers, the over-all effect is to reduce aggregate demand, because rentiers and entrepreneurs tend to have a lower marginal propensity to consume; that is, for each additional dollar they earn, they save a higher percentage than do workers. Obviously, if labour's share of national income declines, there is a definite likelihood that the economy could be caught in a long-term recessionary trap. In fact, over the last twenty years, real wages have been declining in both Canada and the United States, which may go a long way toward explaining the mediocre performance of the economy during this period. Seen in this light, government efforts to reduce the deficit through wage roll-backs and cuts can only undermine the already fragile health of the economy. Ironically, it is by cutting back government spending that we end up creating deficits, not the other way around.

Policy Implications

If the objective of governments is to reduce unemployment or, better yet, to achieve full employment, a number of institutional policies must be put in place in order to prevent other problems from arising. The first thing governments must realize is that lower short-term and long-term interest rates do not comprise a sufficient condition for long-term growth, although they are important. The presence of uncertainty is a dominant feature of a modern capitalist society, and governments must deal with this as a priority. In the past, capitalism has developed many mechanisms to deal with uncertainty. For instance, since decisions to invest and produce are taken *ex ante* and results are achieved only *ex post*, contracts are a way of dealing with the passage of calendar time, since they allow future sale prices and prices of input (labour and other resources) to be known in advance. Monopolistic concentration of market power and long-term wage settlements through collective bargaining are other such mechanisms. We should not conclude from this, however, that uncertainty is thus eliminated. Macro-economic uncertainty, as opposed to micro-economic uncertainty, is still very much at the heart of modern capitalism, and economic theory cannot escape it.

To ensure full employment in an entrepreneurial economic system, entrepreneurs must expect future demand to be sufficiently profitable to encourage them to borrow the funds they need to finance the level of contractual demands that will ensure full employment of resources. Full-employment policies must be linked to the discussion of credit access that was developed in previous chapters. In itself, however, the availability of credit is also not a sufficient condition for the growth of modern economies, because of uncertainty. Economists must also understand how commercial banks operate. Why will banks not simply lend more money? The answer is that banks are like any other private firm: they seek to make profits and grow. When the economy is weak, they are aware that effective demand is also weak, and so investments may not be as profitable. Firms will go bankrupt and the banks will lose their money. The bottom line is that it does not pay for banks to be more "optimistic" than firms. "The essential element is for all banks to walk to the beat of the same drum. If one bank lends more than others . . . it will surely face problems."[31]

The first step that governments must take is to have the political will to forge ahead with policies that may not immediately be accepted by obvious vested interests. However, in the long term, if governments adopt full-employment policies, consumers and firms will have the confidence (through reduced uncertainty) to plan investments and purchases.

In order to avoid inflationary pressures, governments must then convince labour and entrepreneurs that an incomes policy is in their best interest. The key is to tie wage gains to productivity gains, which will be forthcoming through the adoption of new technologies and concrete technical change.

Third, there is a great need for governments actively to promote public spending in key areas of the economy. The discussion of Keynes's "socialization of investment" in chapter three must therefore be brought into the picture. This would commonly be described as an industrial policy that emphasizes and encourages public spending in core sectors of the economy. What should be discouraged are short-term work plans and inefficient subsidies to firms whose sole intention is to carry out unproductive investments. As Keynes noted in the *General Theory*, "A somewhat comprehensive socialization of investment will prove the only means of securing an approximation to full employment."[32]

Fourth, governments need to adopt a consumption-led recovery through an income-redistribution policy that would see labour's share of national income rise, primarily through higher wages or a higher minimum wage. This would generate much-needed stimulus through increased effective demand.

Finally, a tripartite system should not be overlooked. In order for a government's policies to succeed, it must have the voluntary co-operation of labour and business. The over-all objective should not be for all parties to fight over slices of a given size of pie, but to work together to increase the size of pie so that, in the long term, all groups and classes benefit.

Notes

1. Weldon, "Préface," p. 14. Trans. by author.
2. Phillips, "The Relation between Unemployment."
3. See chapter 24 of the *General Theory* (Keynes, *Collected Writings,* vol. 7).
4. Keynes, *Collected Writings,* vol. 12, p. 14.
5. Seccareccia, "An Alternative," p. 43.
6. Ibid., p. 45.
7. Eichner, *Toward a New Economics.*
8. Lavoie, *Foundations of Post-Keynesian,* p. 223.
9. Seccareccia, "An Alternative to Labour-Market Orthodoxy," p. 48.
10. Keynes, *Collected Writings,* vol. 7, p. 14.
11. Piore, "Fragments of a 'Sociological' Theory of Wages," p. 136.
12. Asimakopulos, *Keynes' General Theory,* p. 31, n4.
13. J. Robinson, *Essays in the Theory of Economic Growth.*
14. Seccareccia, "An Alternative," p. 49.
15. Appelbaum, "The Labor Market," p. 37.
16. Knight, *Risk, Uncertainty and Profits.*
17. Keynes, *Collected Writings,* vol. 14, p. 115.
18. Ibid., vol. 12, p. 161.
19. Grellet, "Le principe des avances," pp. 202–3.
20. Kaldor, "Keynesian Economics After Fifty Years," pp. 9–13.
21. Keynes, *Collected Writings,* vol. 12, p. 163.
22. Ibid., vol. 12, p. 46.
23. Asimakopulos, *Keynes' General Theory,* p. 38.
24. Keynes, *Collected Writings,* vol. 12, p. 148.
25. See OECD, *Full Employment.*
26. Seccareccia, "An Alternative to Labour-Market Orthodoxy," p. 50.
27. Keynes, *Collected Writings,* vol. 26, p. 37.
28. Kaldor, *The Scourge of Monetarism,* p. 61.
29. See Rochon, "Le plein emploi."
30. To name just a few, Bellemare and Simon, "Le défi du plein emploi"; McCallum and Barber, *Controlling Inflation;* Olson, *The Rise and Decline of Nations.*
31. Le Bourva, "Création de la monnaie," p. 34.
32. Keynes, *Collected Writings,* vol. 7, p. 378.

C H A P T E R   S I X

SOME FINAL THOUGHTS
ON THE IMPACT OF NEOCLASSICAL THEORY
AND NEOCONSERVATIVE POLICIES

Canadians are well aware of some of the consequences of the last fifteen years of neoconservative policies. The most obvious effects have been high interest rates, high unemployment, a high unproductive debt, and uneven distribution of income and wealth. While these problems are serious in themselves, there are other issues that are far more fundamental and just as threatening to Canadian society.

Governments and policy makers have a tendency to believe that competitive markets and forces can bring nothing but positive results. In high schools, colleges, and universities, students are taught that perfectly competitive markets are the ideal economic structure, ensuring low prices so that consumers benefit. Monopolies and oligopolies are considered inefficient. It is therefore no surprise to see neoconservative policies based exclusively on competition. In the last ten years, for instance, governments have been busy in the areas of privatization, deregulation, and free trade. However, increased competition may not be beneficial to the over-all economy, although it may bring increased benefits to some segments and groups.

Canada's performance from 1940 to the early 1970s was impressive: employment was strong and the economy produced "good" jobs; wage increases were accompanied by productivity gains, and the over-all standard of living was on the rise. This unprecedented growth led to the emergence of an increasing number of Canadians having access to middle-level incomes; thus, the middle class was expanding. The same cannot be said about the last twenty-odd years. In fact, it can be argued that the reverse has been happening:

real wages have declined, productivity has slowed to a trickle, and over-all profits have declined in Canada and in many other industrial countries, including the United States, England, Germany, and Japan. In Canada, corporate profits before taxes, as a percentage of net domestic income, have declined considerably: in 1980, they stood at 16.1 per cent; today, they are at only 6.2 per cent.[1] The consequences of this decline are significant, and have been felt mainly by workers.

While profits are not the only objective of firms, they are an essential component, since they are an important element of wealth. In recent years, firms have sought to reverse the trend of declining profits, especially in the face of increased globalization of markets. Essentially, firms can increase their profits in only two ways: increasing revenues or cutting costs. One way to increase revenues is to raise prices, a move that firms must be able to justify. In an increasingly global economy, firms can sell their commodities at a higher price, provided the commodity is of better quality. We certainly do not hesitate to buy Sony Walkmans, despite their ridiculously high price. Foreign cars are on average more expensive than American-built cars, but consumers will choose to buy them because they are of better quality. Of course, higher-quality commodities imply that firms are willing to invest in research and development and in training their labour force. However, in Canada, this is not being done. Our over-all commitment to research and development and labour training is among the lowest in the world. There are many reasons that firms may not wish to invest in such areas, but the dominant reasons are that R&D and training are expensive and the benefits are reaped only some time in the future. In general, there is so much uncertainty regarding the future that firms are reluctant to invest in their ventures. Why would entrepreneurs plan expensive investments when they do not even know if they will remain in business? After all, bankruptcy rates have never been so high.

As firms refuse to choose the route of better product quality in order to increase profits, they turn to cost-cutting measures that can bring them higher short-run profits. This is where the danger lies. The dominant component of production costs is wages, and firms are not hesitant to cut them or roll them back. More and more, firms are looking at labour quantity and costs as flexible elements that can be increased and decreased at will. Thus, firms have decided to become more competitive by lowering wages, rather than by investing in productive capital. In the end, unproductive and uncompetitive firms are allowed to survive, and they fall so far behind that they can no longer afford to upgrade their production lines.

The search for flexibility has had tremendous consequences, which we only rarely hear about. One of these is what has been termed the rise of the contingent labour force:[2] firms are turning to part-time or temporary workers in order to reduce wages. Since these workers are generally not unionized, firms can pay them less than they would permanent full-time unionized workers—in some cases, up to a third less. The savings can be enormous. In Canada, statistics show that contingent labour now represents one third of all jobs in Canada, while it accounted for less than one quarter fifteen years ago. While part-time work accounted for 4 per cent of all jobs in 1953, it now represents 17 per cent. Since 1975, it has accounted for 30 per cent of all new jobs, for a growth rate of 6.3 per cent. In comparison, the number of permanent jobs grew at the rate of only 1.3 per cent over the same period.

These facts are important as the economy prepares to enter the upward part of its cycle. While there may be some improvement on the employment front, we must ask ourselves what kind of jobs are being created. Are they "good" jobs or "bad" jobs? Since the recession began, in 1990, the number of part-time jobs has climbed by 286,000, while the number of full-time jobs has plunged by 455,000. Similarly, during the years of prosperity of 1981–86, half of the new jobs were low-paying contingent jobs. The consequences for an economy that depends on demand are quite obvious: low-paying jobs mean a generally lower level of effective demand, which dampens any hope of a strong economic recovery.

Many economists point out that firms have always relied on contingent labour. The difference, however, is that in the past firms hired and part-time employees to respond to temporary fluctuations in demand (responding by increasing production), while today they incorporate contingent labour into their employment strategies. Labour—and labour income—thus becomes an extremely variable input of production.

If we add to this the great increase in the service sector, in which workers are paid much less than workers in manufacturing and construction, the over-all results are worrisome. The growth of the service sector is not necessarily bad, as long as it can sustain the growth in wages and in the standard of living. This has not, however, in general been the case.

While 60 per cent of the labour force worked in the industrial sector in 1940, this proportion has fallen dramatically, to only 18 per cent today. The decline has been gradual until recently. From 1911 to 1951, the proportion of Canadian workers in the service sector grew from 34 per cent to 44 per cent, for an annual growth rate of 0.25 per cent. From 1967 to 1988, however, the annual growth rate was 3.2 per cent, compared to the industrial sector, where the growth rate was only 0.9 per cent over the same period. Since 1967, 90 per cent of all new jobs in Canada have been in the service-oriented sector, and today, more than 71 per cent of the labour force is directly associated with this sector. Given that the average wage of workers in the service sector is up to a third lower than that of workers in the industrial sector, the stagnation of the economy in the last decade (along with reduced government spending) can be directly explained by the fall of effective demand.

Expansion of the service sector and reliance on increased competition as an economic objective have led to what has been called the "decline of the middle class": because our economies have lost the capacity to continue with progress toward a more equitable society, there is a trend is toward an increasing polarization of incomes.[3] An increasing number of workers have either very high or very low incomes; fewer and fewer are in the middle bracket.

In Canada, some studies have shown the same trend. Depending on the study, the middle class has shrunk by anywhere from 5.3 per cent to 8 per cent since 1967.[4] Most of the decline has taken place at the lower end of the income-distribution scale.

From a purely economic standpoint, the decline of the middle class is of little concern, since markets can eventually refocus their production to adapt to emerging new consumer demands. Firms would produce more commodities suited for lower-income earners, more luxury commodities suited for higher-income earners, and fewer middle-class consumer durables. But economics is more than just an efficient allocation of resources; it is about our standard of living, about a just and equitable distribution of income, and about social justice. As I have pointed out throughout this book, there is a need to go beyond the pure mathematical logic of economics to see the larger social, historical, and institutional picture.

Whether or not we see the increase in income polarization as detrimental depends on our vision of society and of the world—on whether we believe that a more equitable distribution of income and gains is a socially desirable goal. The importance of the middle class has a special significance in the history of economics. We can recall Marx's apocalyptic warnings that capitalism could create such a bipolar distribution of income that the poor would eventually revolt against the bourgeois and install a communist regime. Of course, I am not suggesting that Marx's prediction will come true—people are too complacent—but there is an argument to be made for the increasing importance of the middle class in a healthy democratic capitalist system. The middle class has a vested interest in preserving the system, and its strong presence ensures the stability the system so badly needs. While we can put aside Marx's doom and gloom, we cannot ignore the fact that the decline of the middle class may create severe problems in the long run.

Famous Last Words

In the concluding paragraph of the *General Theory*, Keynes assumed that the economic nightmare of the 1930s would compel governments to change their economic policies and strategies. The parallels with today's economic problems cannot be overlooked. What is surprising is governments' persistence in following the same policies that led us into this mess in the first place. The politics of austerity, championed by neoconservatives, are bound to give us nothing but increasing strife. Keynes, too, had great disdain for conservatism. He once asked, "How could I bring myself to be a conservative? . . . They offer me neither food nor drink—neither intellectual nor spiritual consolation. . . . It leads nowhere; it satisfies no ideal; it conforms to no intellectual standard; it is not even safe, or calculated to preserve from spoilers that degree of civilization which we have already attained."[5] A few years before, he referred to neoconservative policies as "a sort of mystical stupidity."[6]

The policies adopted and the economic objectives pursued over the last fifteen years have simply been wrong; they have not met their objectives—or if they have, the price has been too great. There is therefore a need—a great need—to rethink how an entrepreneurial economy works. There is a need to adopt new policies that reflect the true functioning of the real world, and not that of some utopia. Life is not orderly, and economic policy should not pretend that it is.

It is perhaps fitting to end this book the same way I began: by reminding readers that economics is in a state of crisis both in theory and in practice and that there has been, as Keynes has said, "a fundamental misunderstanding of how our economy works." An alternative is needed, and this book offers a beginning. For Keynes's revolution to succeed, governments must first be convinced that Canadians are ready to accept new ideas. The purpose of this book was to show that alternatives do exist. I hope that it will be followed by many more, which will explore in greater detail some of the ideas presented herein. Heterodox economists have a special responsibility, given the circumstances, to show that there are alternative approaches that form an "intergral whole."

Are Canadians ready to accept new ideas? Are we prepared to try more humane policies that would benefit the greater community more than the selected few? After more than a decade of unimpressive economic growth, with high unemployment, high real interest rates, and unproductive speculative investments, Canadians may be on the verge of accepting alternative economic policies. Economics is not an end in itself, but a way of attaining the ethical and moral objectives that we set ourselves. The history of capitalism has been just that: an accommodation of the values we share. We must now go much farther; this may be the greatest challenge of economic policy. Economists should perhaps concentrate less on mathematical sophistication and a bit more on the philosophical and social foundations of modern societies. Keynes wrote, "At the present moment people are unusually expectant of a more fundamental diagnosis; more particularly ready to receive it, eager to try it out, if it should be even plausible."[7] His words ring true even today.

Notes

1. Statistics Canada, *National Income and Expenditure Accounts, Catalogue 13-201, Annual Estimates 1980–1991*, p. 84, table 6.2.
2. Bluestone and Harrison, *The Deindustrialization of America.*
3. Kuttner, "The Declining Middle."
4. See Bradbury, "The Shrinking Middle Class"; Drache, *The Deindustrialization of Canada.*; and Picot, *Les bons emplois.*
5. Keynes, *Collected Writings,* vol. 9, pages 296–97.
6. Ibid., vol. 19, p. 144.
7. Ibid., vol. 12, p. 383.

BIBLIOGRAPHY

Abele, Francis, ed. *How Ottawa Spends 1992–1993: The Politics of Competitiveness.* Toronto: Lorimer, 1993.

Appelbaum, Eileen. "The Labor Market in Post-Keynesian Theory." In Michael Piore, ed., *Unemployment & Inflation: Institutionalist and Structuralist Views,* pp. 33–45. New York: M.E. Sharpe, 1979.

Arestis, Philip, and Victoria Chick, eds. *Recent Developments in Post-Keynesian Economics.* Eldershot: Edward Elgar, 1982.

Asimakopulos, Athanasios. "The Determination of Investment in Keynes's Model." *Canadian Journal of Economics,* 4 (Aug. 1970): 382–88.

—. "Keynes's Theory of Effective Demand Revisited." *Australian Economic Papers,* 21 (June 1982): 18–36.

—. "The Nature and Role of Equilibrium in Keynes's *General Theory.*" *Australian Economic Papers* (June 1989): 16–28.

—. *Keynes's General Theory and Accumulation.* Cambridge: Cambridge University Press, 1991.

Bellan, Ruben. "Les déficits budgétaires fédéraux : Quels fardeaux ? Quels dangers ?" In Pierre Paquette and Mario Seccareccia, eds., *Les pièges de l'austérité—dette nationale et prospérité économique : alternatives à l'orthodoxie,* 41–60. Montreal: Presses de l'Université de Montréal, 1993.

Bellemare, Diane, and Lise Poulin Simon. *Le défi du plein emploi: un nouveau regard économique.* Montreal: Éditions St-Martin, 1986.

Bernstein, Peter. "All the Things Deficits Don't Do." *Wall Street Journal,* 10 Nov. 1988.

Bluestone, Barry, and Bennett Harrison. *The Deindustrialization of America.* New York: Basic Books, 1982.

Bonin, Bernard. "L'analyse économique et les effets du libre-échange." In *ACFAS, un marché, deux sociétés?,* Proceedings of the 54th Conference of AFCAS, May 1986. Edited by Pierre G. Hamel. 9–16. Montreal: Université de Montréal, 1987.

Bradbury, Katherine. "The Shrinking Middle Class." *New England Economic Review*, (Sept. 1986): 1–32.

Carvalho, F. "On the Concept of Time in Shacklean and Sraffian Economics." *Journal of Post Keynesian Economics* 6, no. 2 (1984): 265–80.

Chorney, Harold, John Hotson, and Mario Seccareccia. *The Deficit Made Me Do It: The Myths about Government Debt.* Ottawa: Centre for Policy Alternatives, 1992.

Coulombe, Serge. *La dynamique de la dette publique du gouvernement fédéral canadien : le diagnostic d'un problème.* University of Ottawa, mimeo, 1989.

Cornwall, John. *The Conditions for Economic Recovery: A Post-Keynesian Analysis.* Armonk, NY: M.E. Sharpe, 1983.

Cripps, F. "The Money Supply, Wages and Inflation." *Cambridge Journal of Economics*, 1, no. 1 (1977): 101–12.

Cyert, R.M., and H.A. Simon. "The Behavioral Approach: With Emphasis on Economics." *Behavioral Science*, 28, no. 1 (1983): 95–108.

Davidson, Paul. *Money and the Real World.* London: MacMillan, 1972.

—. "Post Keynesian Economics: Solving the Crisis in Economic Theory." In Daniel Bell and Irving Kristol, eds., *The Crisis in Economic Theory*, 151–73. New York: Basic Books, 1981.

—. *Controversies in Post Keynesian Theory.* Eldershot: Edward Elgar, 1991.

DeVroey, Michel. "The Transition from Classical to Neoclassical Economics: A Scientific Revolution." *Journal of Economic Issues* 9, no. 3 (Sept. 1975): 415–39.

Dow, Sheila. *Macroeconomic Thought: A Methodological Approach.* Oxford: Basil Blackwell, 1985.

Dow, Sheila C., and Peter E. Earl. "Methodology and Orthodox Monetary Policy." *Économie appliquée*, 37, no. 1 (1984): 143–64.

Drache, Daniel. *The Deindustrialization of Canada and Its Implications for Labour.* Ottawa: Centre for Policy Alternatives, 1989.

Duesenberry, James S. *Business Cycles and Economic Growth.* New York: McGraw-Hill, 1958.

Dutt, A.K. "Rentiers in Post-Keynesian Models." in Philip Arestis and Victoria Chick, eds., *Recent Developments in Post Keynesian Economics,* 95–122. Eldershot: Edward Elgar, 1992.

Eichner, Alfred. *The Megacorp and the Oligopoly: Micro Foundations of Macro Dynamics.* Cambridge: Cambridge University Press, 1976.

—. *Toward a New Economics: Essays in Post-Keynesian and Institutionalist Theory.* London: MacMillan, 1986.

—. *The Macrodynamics of Advanced Market Economics.* New York: M.E. Sharpe, 1987.

Eichner, Alfred, and J.A. Kregel. "An Essay in Post-Keynesian Theory: A New Paradigm in Economics." *Journal of Economic Literature,* 13, no. 4 (Dec. 1975): 1293–1311.

Eisner, Robert. "Budget Deficits: Rhetoric and Reality." *Journal of Economic Perspectives,* 3, no. 2 (1989): 73–94.

Fitzgibbons, Athol. "From Keynes's Vision to Keynesian Economics." In Philip Arestis and Victoria Chick, eds., *Recent Developments in Post-Keynesian Economics,* 17–26. Eldershot: Edward Elgar, 1992.

Friedman, Benjamin. *Day of Reckoning.* New York: Random House, 1988.

Friedman, Milton. *Essays in Positive Economics.* Chicago: University of Chicago Press, 1953.

—. "A Theoretical Framework for Monetary Analysis." In R.J. Gordon, ed., *Milton Friedman's Monetary Framework: A Debate with His Critics,* 1–62. Chicago: University of Chicago Press, 1974.

Friedman, Milton, and Anna Schwartz. *A Monetary History of the United States, 1867-1960.* Princeton: Princeton University Press, 1963.

Galbraith, J.K. *Economics and the Public Purpose.* Boston: Houghton Mifflin, 1973.

Gerrard, Bill. "Human Logic in Keynes's Thought: Escape from the Cartesian Vice." In Philip Arestis and Victoria Chick, eds., *Recent Developments in Post-Keynesian Economics,* 1–6. Eldershot: Edward Elgar, 1992.

Grellet, G. "Le principe des avances et la théorie keynésienne de l'emploi." In Alain Barrère, ed., *Controverses sur le système keynésien,* 194–203. Paris: Economica, 1976.

Guerrien, B. *Concurrence, flexibilité et stabilité.* Paris: Economica, 1989.

Harrod, Roy. "Note on A Treatise on Probability." Appendix to *The Life of John Maynard Keynes.* London: Macmillan, 1951.

Hayek, Friedrich. *Individualism and Economic Order.* Chicago: University of Chicago Press, 1948.

Heilbroner, Robert, and Peter Bernstein. *The Debt and the Deficit: False Alarms/Real Possibilities.* New York: W.W. Norton, 1989.

Henry, John. "On Equilibrium." *Journal of Post-Keynesian Economics* 6, no. 2 (1984): 214–229.

Hicks, John. *The Crisis in Keynesian Economics.* Oxford: Basil Blackwell, 1974.

—. *Economic Perspectives.* Oxford: Oxford University Press, 1977.

—. *Causality in Economics.* New York: Basic Books, 1979.

—. "ISLM—An Explanation." *Journal of Post Keynesian Economics,* 3 (1981): 139–54.

Hyams, E. *New Statesmanship.* London: Longmans, 1963.

Kaldor, Nicholas. "The Irrelevance of Equilibrium in Economics." *Economic Journal* 82 (1972): 1237–1255.

—. *The Scourge of Monetarism.* Oxford: Oxford University Press, 1982.

—. "Keynesian Economics After Fifty Years." In D. Worswick and T. Trevithick, eds., *Keynes and the Modern World,* 1–28. Cambridge: Cambridge University Press, 1983.

—. *Economics without Equilibrium.* Armonk, NY: M.E. Sharpe, 1985.

Kenyon, Peter. "Pricing." In A. Eichner, ed., *A Guide to Post-Keynesian Economics*, pp. 34–45. New York: M.E. Sharpe, 1979.

Keynes, John Maynard. *The Collected Writings of John Maynard Keynes*, London: Macmillan, St. Martin's Press and Cambridge University Press, 1973. Edited by Donald Moggridge for the Royal Economic Society. Vol. 6, *A Treatise on Money 2: The Applied Theory of Money* (1930); vol. 7, *The General Theory of Employment, Interest and Money* (1936); vol. 9, *Essays in Persuasion* (1931); vol. 13, *The General Theory and After: Part I Preparation*; vol. 14, *The General Theory and After: Part II Defence and Development;* vol. 21, *Activities 1931–1939: World Crises and Policies in Britain and America;* vol. 26, *Activities 1941–1946: Shaping the Post-War World: Bretton Woods and Reparations;* vol. 27, *Activities 1940–1946: Shaping the Post-War World: Employment and Commodities;* vol. 28, *Social, Political and Literary Writings;* vol. 29, *The General Theory and After: A Supplement.*

Knight, Frank. *Risk, Uncertainty and Profit*. 1921. New York: Augustus M. Kelley, 1964.

Koutsoyiannis, Anna. *Modern Microeconomics, Second Edition*. London: MacMillan, 1983.

Kregel, J.A. "Monetary Production Economics and Monetary Policy." *Économies et Sociétés*, 18, no. 4 (1984): 221–32.

Kuttner, Robert. "The Declining Middle," *Atlantic Monthly*, July, 1983, 12–21.

Latsis, S.J., ed. *Method and Appraisal in Economics*. Cambridge: Cambridge University Press, 1976.

Lavoie, Marc. "La distinction entre l'incertitude keynésienne et le risque néoclassique." *Économie appliquée*, 38, no. 2 (1985a): 493–518.

—. "Credit and Money: The Dynamic Circuit, Overdraft Economics, and Post-Keynesian Economics." In M. Jarsulic, ed., *Money and Macro Policy*, 63–84. Boston: Kluwer-Nijhoff, 1985b.

—. "Towards a New Research Programme for Post-Keynesianism and Neo-Ricardinism." *Review of Political Economy,* 4, no. 1 (1992a): 37–78.

—. *Foundations of Post-Keynesian Economic Analysis.* Eldershot: Edward Elgar, 1992b.

—. "L'idéologie des discours budgétaires fédéraux : plus ça change, plus c'est pareil." In Pierre Paquette and Mario Seccareccia, eds., *Les pièges de l'austérité—Dette nationale et prospérité économique : alternatives à l'orthodoxie,* 105–30. Montreal: Presses de l'université de Montréal, 1993.

Lavoie, Marc, and Mario Seccareccia, eds. *Milton et son œuvre.* Les grands penseurs series. Montreal: Presses de l'université de Montréal, 1993.

Lawson, Tony. "Uncertainty and Economic Analysis in Economics." *The Economic Journal,* 95 (1985): 909–27.

Leimer, G. "Let's Take the Con out of Econometrics." *American Economic Review,* 73 (1983): 31–43.

Le Bourva, Jacques. "Création de la monnaie et multiplicateur du crédit." *Revue Économique,* 13, no. 1 (Jan. 1962): 29–56.

Marshall, Alfred. *Principles of Economics.* 1890. 9th ed. (variorum), annotated by C.W. Guillebaud. New York: Macmillan Company, 1961.

—. *Principles of Economics.* 1890. 8th ed. London: MacMillan, 1920.

McCallum, John, and Clarence Barber. *Controlling Inflation: Learning from Experience in Canada, Europe and Japan.* Toronto: Lorimer, 1982.

Means, G.C. "The Administered-Price Thesis Reconfirmed." *American Economic Review,* 61 (1972): 292–306.

Minsky, Hyman P. *John Maynard Keynes,* New York: Columbia University Press, 1975.

Moore, Basil. *Horizontalists and Verticalists: The Macroeconomics of Credit Money.* Cambridge: Cambridge University Press, 1988.

—. "The Endogeneity of Money Once More." *Journal of Post Keynesian Economics*, 11, no. 3 (Spring 1989): 479–487.

Munnel, Alicia. "Is There Too Little Public Capital." *The Public's Capital* 2 (1991).

Myrdal, Gunnar. *The Political Element in the Development of Economic Theory*. Trans. Paul Streeten. Cambridge, MA: Harvard University Press, 1954.

—. *Objectivity in Social Research*. New York: Pantheon, 1969.

Nell, E. "The Revival of Political Economy." *Social Research*, 39, no. 1 (1972). Rpt. in *Transformational Growth and Effective Demand*, 8–22. New York: NYU Press, 1991.

O'Donnel, John. *Keynes: Philosophy, Economics and Politics, the Philosophical Foundations of Keynes's Thought and Their Influence on His Economics and Politics*. New York: St. Martin's Press, 1989.

O'Donnel, Rod. "The Unwritten Books and Papers of J.M. Keynes." *History of Political Economy*, 24, no. 4 (1992).

OECD. *Full Employment and Growth as the Social and Economic Goal*. Paris, 1986.

Olson, Mankur. *The Rise and Decline of Nations: Economic Growth, Stagflation and Social Rigidities*. New Haven: Yale University Press, 1982.

Penner, Rudolph. "The Economics and the Morality of the Budget Deficit." *Business Economics*, October, 1988, 6–12.

Peterson, Wallace. "Institutionalism, Keynes and the Real World." *Journal of Economic Issues*, 11, no. 2 (1977): 201–22.

Phillips, A.W. "The Relation between Unemployment and the Rate of Change of Money Wage Rates in the United Kingdom, 1861–1957." *Economica*, 25 (1958): 283–319.

Picot, Garnet. *Les bons emplois et les mauvais emplois et le déclin de la classe moyenne : 1967–1986*. Ottawa: Statistics Canada, 1990.

Piore, Michael. "Fragments of a 'Sociological' Theory of Wages." In Michael Piore, ed., *Unemployment and Inflation: Institution-*

alist and Structuralist Views, pp. 5–16. White Plains, NY: M. E. Sharpe, 1979.

Robinson, Austin. "Could There Have Been a 'General Theory' without Keynes?" In Robert Lekachman, ed., Keynes's General Theory: Reports of Three Decades, 87–95. New York: St. Martin's Press, 1964.

Robinson, Joan. Economics of Imperfect Competition. London: Macmillan, 1933.

—. Essays in the Theory of Economic Growth. London: MacMillan, 1962a.

—. Economic Philosophy. Chicago: Aldine Publishing Company, 1962b.

—. Introduction to the Theory of Employment. London: MacMillan, 1969.

—. Collected Economic Papers. Vol. 4. Oxford: Basil Blackwell, 1973.

—. The Contribution of Keynes to Economic Theory. Lecture given at Carleton University, Ottawa, 1974.

—. "What are the Questions?" Journal of Economic Literature, 15, no. 4 (1977)

—. Collected Economic Papers. Vol. 5. Oxford: Basil Blackwell, 1980.

Rochon, Louis-Philippe. "Le plein emploi : une politique sociale . . . et économique." Cité libre, Sept. 1991.

—. "Le partenariat social." Cité libre, October, 1991b.

—. "La mondialisation et les nouvelles missions de l'État." In Louis-Philippe Rochon and Angéline Fournier, eds., Thèses ou Foutaise : Défis pour une nouvelle génération. Montreal: L'Étincelle Éditeur, 1992.

—. "Le syndicalisme et le mythe de l'improductivité." Cité libre, March, 1992.

Roncaglia, A. Sraffa and the Theory of Prices. New York: John Wiley, 1978.

Rousseas, Stephen. Post Keynesian Monetary Economics. New York: M.E. Sharpe, 1986.

Russel, Robert. *Fallacies of Monetarism. Western Michigan University, 1981.*

Samuels, Warren J. "Truth and Discourse in the Social Construction of Economic Reality." *Journal of Post Keynesian Economics,* 13 (Summer 1991): 512–24.

Sawyer, M.C. *The Challenge of Radical Political Economy.* London: Harvester Whearsheaf, 1989.

Schumpeter, J.A. *Ten Great Economists from Marx to Keynes.* London: G. Allen and Unwin, 1952.

Seccareccia, Mario. *Post-Keynesian Fundism and Monetary Circulation.* Mimeo, No. 9113E, University of Ottawa, 1991a.

—. "An Alternative to Labour-Market Orthodoxy: the Post-Keynesian/Institutionalist Policy View." *Review of Political Economy,* 3, no. 1 (1991b): 43–61.

—. *Keynesianism and Public Investment: Re-Evaluating Social-Democratic Goals Within a Left-Keynesian Perspective.* Mimeo, University of Ottawa, 1993.

Seccareccia, Mario, and Marc Lavoie. "Les idées révolutionnaires de Keynes en politique et le déclin du capitalisme rentier." *Économie appliquée,* 12, no. 1 (1989): 47–70.

Seccareccia, Mario and Andrew Sharpe. "Déficits budgétaires et compétitivité du Canada : une analyse critique." In Pierre Paquette and Mario Seccareccia, eds., *Les pièges de l'austérité—dette nationale et prospérité économique: alternatives à l'orthodoxie,* 131–54. Montreal: Presses de l'université de Montréal, 1993.

Shackle, G.L.S. *Keynesian Kaleidics.* Edinburgh: Edinburgh University Press, 1974.

—. *Time, Expectations and Uncertainty in Economics.* Ed. by J.L. Ford. Albershot: Edward Elgar.

—. "Sir John Hicks' 'IS-LM: An Explanation': A Comment." *Journal of Post Keynesian Economics,* 4 (1982): 435–38.

Shannon, R., and M. Wallace. "Wages and Inflation: An Investigation into Causality." *Journal of Post Keynesian Economics,* 8, no. 2 (1986): 182–91.

Shapiro, N. (1977). "The Revolutionary Character of Post-Keynes-ian Economics." *Journal of Economic Issues,* 9 no. 3 (Sept. 1977): 541–60.

Sherman, Howard. "The Sad State of Orthodox Economics." *Journal of Economic Issues,* 9, no. 2 (June 1975): 243–50.

Simon, Herbert. "From Substantive to Procedural Rationality." In S.J. Latsis, ed., *Method and Appraisal in Economics,* 129–48. Cambridge: Cambridge University Press, 1976.

Spencer, R.W., and W.P. Yoke. "The 'Crowding-Out' Effect of Private Expenditures by Fiscal Policy Actions. *Federal Reserve Bank of St. Louis Review* (1970).

Sraffa, Pierro. "The Laws of Return under Competitive Conditions." *Economic Journal,* 36 (1926): 535–50.

Tobin, James. "Theoretical Issues in Macroeconomics." In G.R. Feiwel, ed., *Issues in Contemporary Macroeconomics and Distribution,* 103–33. Albany: State University of New York Press, 1985.

Vicarelli, Fausto. *Keynes, The Instability of Capitalism.* Philadelphia: University of Pennsylvania Press, 1984.

Weldon, Jack. "Préface." In Diane Bellemare and Lise Poulin Simon, *Le défi du plein emploi : un nouveau regard économique,* 9–18. Montreal: St-Martin, 1988.

Weintraub, Jack. "Uncertainty and the Keynesian Revolution." *History of Political Economy,* 7, no. 4 (Winter 1975): 530–48.

Winslow, E.G. "Organic Interdependence, Uncertainty and Economic Analysis." *Economic Journal,* 99 (Dec. 1989): 1173–82.

Wray, Randall. "L'effet d'éviction et les déficits budgétaires aux États-Unis." In Pierre Paquette and Mario Seccareccia eds., *Les pièges de l'austérité—dette nationale et prospérité économique : alternatives à l'orthodoxie,* 61–77. Montreal: Presses de l'Université de Montréal, 1993.

PRINTED IN CANADA